Be The Man She Needs

Malcolm Carter

Published by Defenestration Press, 2024.

BE THE MAN SHE NEEDS

First edition. September 8, 2024.

Copyright © 2024 Malcolm Carter.

ISBN: 979-8224153831

Written by Malcolm Carter.

Table of Contents

Understanding Love Beyond Words 1

The Power of Active Listening 9

Understanding Her Love Language 21

The Importance of Emotional Vulnerability 33

Showing Up Every Day 43

The Art of Appreciation 53

Rekindling the Romance 63

Supporting Her Dreams 72

Navigating Conflict with Grace 82

Cultivating Patience and Understanding 93

Building Trust Through Transparency 102

Sharing Responsibilities 112

Prioritizing Intimacy 122

The Joy of Giving Without Expecting 130

Growing Together, Not Apart 139

Understanding Love Beyond Words

Love is a word we all know, but how many of us truly understand its depth, its power, and its real meaning, especially within the sacred bond of marriage? When you think about love, what comes to mind? Maybe it's the butterflies you felt on your first date, or the way your heart races when you see your wife smile. These feelings are a beautiful part of love, no doubt, but they're just the tip of the iceberg.

We're going to dive deep. We're going to look beyond the surface and explore what love truly means in a marriage. Because, brothers, it's not just about saying "I love you." It's about living that love every single day, through your actions, your thoughts, and your choices.

I'm going to be real with you: This isn't easy. It takes work, commitment, and a willingness to grow. But here's the thing—if you're willing to put in that work, the love you'll cultivate in your marriage will be deeper, richer, and more fulfilling than you ever imagined. So let's get started.

The Myth of "I Love You"

"I love you." Three little words that carry so much weight. We're taught from a young age that these words are the ultimate expression of our feelings for someone. And while it's important to say "I love you," we can't let those words do all the heavy lifting. Because love—real, true love—isn't just about what you say. It's about what you do.

Let me tell you a story. I once worked with a couple who had been married for 15 years. They were struggling, and the wife felt like her husband didn't love her anymore. When I asked the husband about it, he was shocked. "I tell her I love her all the time," he said. "How could she not know?"

But here's the thing: While he was saying "I love you," his actions were telling a different story. He wasn't showing up for her in the ways she needed. He was busy with work, distracted at home, and not really engaged in their relationship. His words said one thing, but his actions said another. And over time, those words started to lose their meaning.

This isn't uncommon. We can get so caught up in the routine of life that we forget to actively show our love. We say the words out of habit, but we don't back them up with action. And that's where the disconnect happens.

Redefining Love: What Does It Really Mean?

So, what does love really mean in a marriage? It's a big question, and there isn't one simple answer. But I'll tell you this: Love is a verb. It's something you do, not just something you feel or say. It's an ongoing, active choice you make every day.

Let's break that down a bit.

1. Love is Respect.

At its core, love is about respect. It's about seeing your wife as an equal partner, valuing her thoughts, her feelings, and her contributions. It's about listening to her, not just hearing her. It's about recognizing her worth and treating her with the dignity she deserves.

Respect isn't just about the big things, like supporting her career or sharing household responsibilities—though those are crucial. It's also about the small things, like how you speak to her, how you react when she's upset, and how you make her feel valued every day.

Ask yourself: Do I show my wife the respect she deserves? Am I treating her with kindness, patience, and understanding? Because without respect, love can't thrive.

2. Love is Presence.

In today's world, it's easy to be physically present but mentally absent. We're glued to our phones, distracted by work, or caught up in our own thoughts. But love requires more than just being in the same room. It requires presence—real, engaged, focused presence.

Being present means giving your wife your full attention when she's talking to you. It means putting down your phone, turning off the TV, and really being there with her. It means being attuned to her needs, noticing when she's feeling down or stressed, and responding with care.

When you're truly present, you're showing your wife that she matters more than anything else in that moment. And that's a powerful expression of love.

3. Love is Action.

As I mentioned earlier, love is a verb. It's about what you do, not just what you say. This means showing your love through your actions—both big and small.

Love is making her morning coffee just the way she likes it. It's taking care of the kids so she can have a break. It's planning a date night to show her that you still value your time together. It's being there when she needs you, even if it's inconvenient or challenging.

These actions, no matter how small, add up over time. They create a pattern of love that's felt deeply and consistently. And they show your wife that your love isn't just words—it's real, it's tangible, and it's something she can count on.

4. Love is Understanding.

No two people are the same, and that's what makes relationships so rich and complex. But it also means that understanding each other—really understanding each other—takes work.

Love is about seeking to understand your wife's perspective, even when it's different from your own. It's about being curious about her thoughts, her feelings, and her experiences. It's about asking questions, listening without judgment, and trying to see the world through her eyes.

This kind of understanding doesn't happen overnight. It's something you build over time, through open, honest communication and a willingness to learn from each other. But when you make the effort to truly understand your wife, you're showing her that her inner world matters to you. And that's one of the deepest expressions of love there is.

5. Love is Sacrifice.

Here's the hard truth: Love isn't always easy. Sometimes, it requires sacrifice. It means putting your wife's needs before your own, even when it's difficult. It means making choices that benefit the relationship, even if they're not what you would prefer.

But let me be clear—sacrifice in love isn't about losing yourself or giving up your own needs. It's about finding a balance where both of you can thrive. It's about being willing to compromise, to give a little more when your wife needs it, and to make decisions that support your marriage as a whole.

When you make sacrifices for your wife, you're showing her that your love is selfless, that it's about more than just what you get out of the relationship. You're showing her that you're committed to her happiness, to her well-being, and to the life you're building together.

Moving Beyond Surface-Level Love

So how do you move beyond surface-level love? How do you take these ideas and put them into practice in your daily life?

It starts with a shift in mindset. You have to move from thinking about love as a feeling to thinking about love as a choice. Every day, you have the opportunity to choose love—to choose to be respectful, present, active, understanding, and selfless. And when you make those choices consistently, love becomes a way of life, not just something you talk about.

Here are a few practical steps to help you start living love beyond words:

1. Reflect on Your Actions

Take some time to reflect on how you show love to your wife. Are your actions aligned with your words? Are there areas where you could do more, be more present, or show more understanding? Be honest with yourself, and don't be afraid to acknowledge where you can improve.

2. Communicate Openly

Talk to your wife about what love means to her. Ask her how she feels loved, what makes her feel valued, and where she might need more from you. This conversation can be eye-opening, and it will give you the insight you need to love her in the way she needs most.

3. Be Consistent

Love isn't about grand gestures—it's about the little things you do every day. Make a commitment to show your love consistently, in both small and big ways. Over time, these actions will create a strong foundation of love that's felt deeply and genuinely.

4. Prioritize Your Marriage

In the busyness of life, it's easy to let your marriage take a back seat. But if you want to love your wife deeply and fully, you have to prioritize your relationship. This means making time for each other, staying connected, and investing in your marriage every day.

5. Practice Empathy

Empathy is the ability to understand and share the feelings of another person. It's a crucial component of love, and it requires practice. Make an effort to see things from your wife's perspective, to feel what she's feeling, and to respond with compassion and understanding.

6. Celebrate the Journey

Loving your wife better is a journey, not a destination. Celebrate the progress you make, the small victories, and the ways your relationship grows stronger. Be patient with yourself and with your wife, and remember that love is a lifelong learning process.

The Foundation for Everything That Follows

Understanding love beyond words sets the foundation for everything that follows in this book—and in your marriage. When you commit to loving your wife in this deep, intentional way, you're laying the groundwork for a relationship that's not only strong but also deeply fulfilling for both of you.

This kind of love isn't always easy, and it requires effort, patience, and a willingness to grow. But it's worth it. Because when you love your wife beyond words—when you show her that love through your actions, your presence, and your understanding—you create a bond that's unbreakable.

So, as you move forward, remember this: Love is more than just words. It's a way of life. And when you live that love every day, you'll not only transform your marriage—you'll transform yourself as well.

Keep this in mind as we move into the next chapters. Everything we're going to explore—communication, trust, intimacy—builds on this foundation of love beyond words. So take these ideas to heart, start putting them into practice, and watch how they begin to transform your relationship. You've got this, and I'm here with you every step of the way.

Let's get to work on becoming the man your wife deserves, and the man you aspire to be.

The Power of Active Listening

Communication is at the heart of any successful relationship, especially in marriage. We hear this all the time, right? "Communication is key." But here's the thing—when we talk about communication, we often focus on the talking part. We think about what we're going to say, how we're going to express our feelings, how we're going to get our point across. And while that's important, it's only half the equation.

The other half? Listening. And not just hearing the words that are being spoken, but really, truly listening. Listening with your heart, with your mind, with your full attention. Listening in a way that makes your wife feel understood, valued, and loved. This, my brothers, is where the real magic happens in a relationship.

We're going to dive deep into the power of active listening. I'm going to show you how to move beyond surface-level conversations and connect with your wife on a much deeper level. Because when you master the art of listening, you're not just improving your communication—you're strengthening the very foundation of your marriage.

Why Listening Matters More Than You Think

Let's start with a simple truth: Everyone wants to feel heard. It's a fundamental human need. When someone truly listens to us, it makes us feel seen, understood, and valued. It's a way of saying, "You matter. What you're feeling and experiencing is important to me."

Now, think about your marriage. How often do you listen to your wife in this way? How often do you give her your full, undivided attention when she's talking to you? If you're like most of us, the answer is probably, "Not as often as I should."

And here's why that's a problem. When your wife doesn't feel heard, she might start to feel disconnected, unimportant, or even resentful. Over time, this can create a distance between you—a gap that can be hard to bridge if it's left unchecked. But when you make the effort to really listen, you're showing your wife that she's a priority in your life, that her thoughts and feelings matter to you. And that's powerful.

But listening isn't just about avoiding problems—it's also about deepening your connection. When you listen actively, you're able to understand your wife on a deeper level. You learn more about what makes her tick, what she needs, and what she's going through. This understanding creates intimacy, trust, and a stronger bond between you.

The Difference Between Hearing and Listening

Before we go any further, let's clarify something important: Hearing and listening are not the same thing.

Hearing is passive. It's what happens when sound waves hit your eardrum and your brain registers them as noise. You can hear someone talking without actually paying attention to what they're saying. We've all done it—nodding along while our mind is somewhere else, thinking about work, the game, or what we're going to say next.

Listening, on the other hand, is active. It's a conscious choice to focus on the person speaking, to pay attention to their words, their tone, their body language. It's about being present in the moment, not just physically but mentally and emotionally as well. When you listen actively, you're engaging with the speaker on a deeper level, showing them that you value what they have to say.

The Components of Active Listening

Active listening is a skill, and like any skill, it takes practice. But once you get the hang of it, it can transform your relationship. So, let's break it down into its key components:

1. Presence

The first and most important part of active listening is being present. This means giving your wife your full attention when she's talking to you. Put down your phone, turn off the TV, and focus on her. This might sound simple, but in today's world, where we're constantly distracted, it's harder than it seems.

Being present also means being mentally and emotionally engaged. Don't let your mind wander or start thinking about what you're going to say next. Stay in the moment and focus on what your wife is saying. This kind of presence shows her that she's important to you, that what she's saying matters.

2. Non-Verbal Cues

Communication isn't just about words. In fact, a lot of what we communicate is done through non-verbal cues—our body language, facial expressions, eye contact, and tone of voice.

When you're listening to your wife, pay attention to these cues. They can tell you a lot about how she's feeling and what she's trying to communicate.

For example, if she's talking about something that's upsetting her, her body language might be tense, her voice might be quieter, or she might avoid eye contact. These are all signs that she's feeling vulnerable, and it's important to respond with empathy and understanding.

Your own non-verbal cues are just as important. Make eye contact, nod to show that you're listening, and use open body language. These signals show your wife that you're engaged in the conversation and that you care about what she's saying.

3. Reflective Listening

Reflective listening is a powerful tool that helps you ensure you've understood what your wife is saying and shows her that you're truly listening. It involves paraphrasing or summarizing what she's said and reflecting it back to her. This not only helps clarify her message but also makes her feel heard and understood.

For example, if your wife is talking about a tough day at work, you might say something like, "It sounds like you had a really stressful day. You've been dealing with a lot of pressure." This shows her that you're not just hearing her words—you're understanding her experience.

Reflective listening also gives your wife the opportunity to clarify or elaborate on what she's saying. If you've misunderstood something, she can correct you, and you can both be on the same page.

4. Empathy

Empathy is the ability to understand and share the feelings of another person. It's a crucial part of active listening because it allows you to connect with your wife on an emotional level. When you listen with empathy, you're not just processing information—you're feeling with her.

To practice empathy, try to put yourself in your wife's shoes. Imagine how she's feeling and what she's going through. Respond with kindness and understanding, and let her know that you're there for her, no matter what she's dealing with.

For example, if she's upset about something, instead of trying to fix the problem right away, you might say, "I'm so sorry you're feeling this way. It sounds really hard." Sometimes, just knowing that you understand and care is enough to make her feel better.

5. Avoiding Interruptions

One of the biggest barriers to active listening is the urge to interrupt. We all do it—jumping in with our thoughts, advice, or reactions before the other person has finished speaking. But when you interrupt, you're sending the message that what you have to say is more important than what your wife is saying.

Resist the urge to interrupt. Let your wife finish her thoughts before you respond. If you need to, take a deep breath and remind yourself that your role right now is to listen, not to fix or advise. When you give her the space to express herself fully, she'll feel more comfortable opening up to you in the future.

6. Asking Questions

Asking questions is a great way to show that you're engaged in the conversation and that you care about understanding your wife's perspective. But be careful—this isn't about interrogating her or steering the conversation in a direction you want it to go. It's about asking thoughtful, open-ended questions that encourage her to share more.

For example, instead of asking, "Why didn't you just tell your boss how you feel?" you might ask, "How did that conversation with your boss make you feel?" The first question can come across as judgmental or dismissive, while the second invites her to share her emotions and experiences.

The Impact of Active Listening on Your Marriage

Now that we've broken down the components of active listening, let's talk about the impact it can have on your marriage. Because, trust me, when you start listening to your wife in this way, you'll notice some powerful changes.

1. Deeper Connection

One of the most profound effects of active listening is the deeper connection it creates between you and your wife. When she feels truly heard and understood, it fosters intimacy and trust. She knows that she can come to you with her thoughts, feelings, and concerns, and that you'll be there to listen without judgment.

This deeper connection isn't just about emotional closeness—it also strengthens your bond on a practical level. You'll be more in tune with each other's needs, which means you can support each other more effectively and navigate challenges as a team.

2. Improved Communication

Active listening naturally leads to better communication. When you're truly listening to your wife, you're more likely to understand her perspective, which means fewer misunderstandings and conflicts. And when disagreements do arise, you'll be better equipped to resolve them in a healthy, constructive way.

Improved communication also means that you're more likely to address issues before they become bigger problems. When your wife knows that she can talk to you and that you'll listen, she's more likely to bring up concerns early on, which gives you both the opportunity to work through them together.

3. Increased Emotional Safety

Emotional safety is a critical component of a healthy marriage. It's the feeling that you can be yourself with your partner, without fear of judgment, rejection, or criticism. When you practice active listening, you're creating a safe space for your wife to express herself openly and honestly.

This emotional safety is especially important during difficult conversations. When your wife knows that you're going to listen to her with empathy and understanding, she'll feel more comfortable sharing her vulnerabilities, her fears, and her needs. This level of openness can bring you closer together and strengthen your relationship.

4. A Stronger Sense of Partnership

Marriage is a partnership, and active listening reinforces that sense of partnership. When you listen to your wife with the intention of understanding and supporting her, you're showing her that you're in this together—that you're committed to working through challenges as a team.

This stronger sense of partnership can lead to greater collaboration in all areas of your life, from parenting to managing household responsibilities to making important decisions. When you listen to each other and value each other's perspectives, you're more likely to find solutions that work for both of you.

5. Greater Appreciation and Respect

Finally, active listening fosters greater appreciation and respect in your marriage. When you take the time to listen to your wife, you're showing her that you value her thoughts, her feelings, and her experiences. This, in turn, leads to a deeper sense of respect and appreciation for each other.

This mutual respect is the foundation of a healthy, loving relationship. It's what allows you to weather the storms of life together, knowing that you can count on each other no matter what.

Putting Active Listening into Practice

So, how do you start putting active listening into practice in your marriage? Here are some practical steps to help you get started:

1. Set Aside Time to Talk

In the hustle and bustle of daily life, it's easy to let meaningful conversations fall by the wayside. Make a conscious effort to set aside time each day to talk with your wife. This doesn't have to be a long, formal conversation—just a few minutes of focused, uninterrupted time where you can connect.

Whether it's over your morning coffee, during a walk, or before bed, find a time that works for both of you. The key is to make it a regular part of your routine so that it becomes a habit.

2. Eliminate Distractions

When you're listening to your wife, eliminate distractions. Turn off the TV, put your phone on silent, and focus on her. This shows her that she has your full attention and that you value what she has to say.

If you're in a situation where you can't eliminate distractions (like when you're driving or in a noisy environment), acknowledge it and let her know that you want to talk when you can give her your full attention.

3. Practice Mindfulness

Mindfulness is the practice of being fully present in the moment. When you're listening to your wife, practice mindfulness by focusing on her words, her tone, and her body language. If you notice your mind starting to wander, gently bring it back to the conversation.

Mindfulness also means being aware of your own reactions. If you feel yourself getting defensive or impatient, take a deep breath and remind yourself that your goal is to listen and understand, not to argue or fix.

4. Use Reflective Listening

As we discussed earlier, reflective listening is a powerful tool for active listening. After your wife has spoken, summarize or paraphrase what she's said and reflect it back to her. This not only helps you ensure that you've understood her correctly, but it also shows her that you're truly listening.

For example, you might say, "So, what I'm hearing is that you're feeling overwhelmed at work and you're not sure how to balance everything. Is that right?" This gives her the opportunity to clarify or elaborate if needed.

5. Validate Her Feelings

Validation is about acknowledging your wife's feelings and letting her know that it's okay to feel the way she does. Even if you don't agree with her perspective, you can still validate her emotions.

For example, if she's upset about something that seems minor to you, resist the urge to minimize her feelings. Instead, say something like, "I can see why that would be really frustrating." This shows her that you're not dismissing her emotions and that you care about how she's feeling.

6. Ask Open-Ended Questions

When appropriate, ask open-ended questions to encourage your wife to share more. Open-ended questions can't be answered with a simple "yes" or "no"—they require more thought and elaboration.

For example, instead of asking, "Did you have a good day?" you might ask, "What was the best part of your day?" or "How are you feeling about that situation at work?" These kinds of questions invite deeper conversation and show that you're interested in her thoughts and feelings.

7. Be Patient

Active listening takes practice, and it's okay if you don't get it perfect right away. Be patient with yourself and with your wife as you work on this skill. The important thing is that you're making an effort to listen more deeply and connect more fully.

Over time, as you practice active listening, you'll start to see the positive impact it has on your marriage. Your connection will deepen, your communication will improve, and you'll build a stronger, more resilient relationship.

Listening as an Act of Love

At its core, active listening is an act of love. It's a way of showing your wife that she matters to you, that her thoughts and feelings are important, and that you're committed to understanding her on a deeper level. When you listen with your heart, with empathy, and with full presence, you're not just improving your communication—you're building a stronger, more loving marriage.

Remember, listening isn't about being perfect. It's about being present, being open, and being willing to learn and grow together. So take what you've learned in this chapter and start putting it into practice. Make the choice to listen more deeply, to connect more fully, and to love your wife in a way that goes beyond words.

This is just the beginning, my brothers. As we continue on this journey together, we'll keep building on this foundation, learning more about how to communicate, connect, and love in ways that truly matter. But for now, take a deep breath, and start listening. Your marriage—and your wife—will thank you for it.

Understanding Her Love Language

Fellas, let's talk about love languages. If you're married, in a relationship, or even just trying to get closer to someone you care about, understanding love languages is a game-changer. You see, love isn't just one-size-fits-all. We all have different ways we give and receive love. What makes you feel loved might not be what makes your wife feel loved, and that's where things can get tricky.

So, we're going to break it down. We're going to explore the different love languages and help you figure out how to identify your wife's primary one. Whether it's words of affirmation, acts of service, receiving gifts, quality time, or physical touch, knowing her love language will help you communicate your love in the way she feels it most deeply. This isn't just about making her happy—it's about building a strong, healthy relationship where you both feel connected and appreciated.

What Are Love Languages?

The concept of love languages was first introduced by Dr. Gary Chapman in his book *The Five Love Languages*. It's become a bit of a buzzword in relationships, but the idea is simple and powerful: We all have a primary way of expressing and receiving love, and understanding that language is key to a fulfilling relationship.

Think of it like this—if you're speaking English and your wife is speaking French, you're going to have a hard time understanding each other. You might be saying "I love you" all day long, but if she doesn't understand your language, she's not going to feel that love. The same goes for love languages. If you're expressing love in a way that doesn't resonate with her, she might not feel as loved as you intend.

So, what are these love languages? Let's break them down:

1. Words of Affirmation: Some people feel most loved when they hear words that build them up. Compliments, words of appreciation, and verbal encouragement mean the world to them. If your wife's love language is words of affirmation, telling her she's beautiful, expressing gratitude, or encouraging her in her goals will make her feel cherished.

2. Acts of Service: For some, actions speak louder than words. If your wife's love language is acts of service, she feels loved when you do things to help her out—whether that's taking care of chores, running errands, or just making her life a little easier. It's about showing your love through your actions.

3. Receiving Gifts: Some people feel most loved when they receive thoughtful gifts. It's not about the cost of the gift, but the thought and effort behind it. If your wife's love language is receiving gifts, a small token of appreciation, a surprise, or something that shows you've been thinking about her can mean a lot.

4. Quality Time: For some, nothing says "I love you" like undivided attention. If your wife's love language is quality time, she feels most loved when you spend time together—just the two of you, focused on each other. It's about being present and making her feel like a priority.

5. Physical Touch: Some people feel most loved through physical touch. This doesn't just mean sex—although that's part of it—but also hugs, holding hands, a touch on the shoulder, or just being physically close. If your wife's love language is physical touch, she feels most connected to you when you're physically affectionate.

Each of these love languages is valid and important, but the key is figuring out which one resonates most with your wife. Because when you speak her love language, you're speaking directly to her heart.

Identifying Your Wife's Love Language

Now that we've covered the basics, let's talk about how to identify your wife's love language. This can be a bit tricky, especially if you've been expressing love in your own language rather than hers. But don't worry—I've got some tips to help you figure it out.

1. Observe Her Behavior

One of the best ways to identify your wife's love language is to pay attention to how she expresses love to you. Often, we give love in the way we want to receive it. So, if your wife is always telling you how much she appreciates you, or she lights up when you give her a compliment, her love language might be words of affirmation. If she's always doing things for you—like cooking your favorite meal, running errands, or taking care of the house—she might value acts of service.

Take note of what she does naturally when she's expressing love. This can give you a big clue about what makes her feel loved.

2. Listen to Her Complaints

This might sound counterintuitive, but another way to identify your wife's love language is to listen to what she complains about. When we don't feel loved, we often express it through complaints, even if we don't realize it.

For example, if your wife frequently says, "You never tell me how much you appreciate what I do," she might be craving words of affirmation. If she often says, "I wish you would spend more time with me," quality time might be her love language. Complaints can be a window into what's missing in the relationship, so pay attention.

3. Ask Her Directly

Sometimes, the best way to find out your wife's love language is to just ask her. You don't have to make it complicated—just have an honest conversation about it. You can ask questions like, "What makes you feel most loved by me?" or "When do you feel the closest to me?" This can open up a dialogue where you both share what you need to feel loved.

You can also take the Love Languages Quiz together. This quiz, based on Dr. Gary Chapman's work, can help both of you identify your primary love languages. It's a great way to learn more about each other and start the conversation about how you can better meet each other's needs.

4. Experiment with Different Languages

If you're still not sure what your wife's love language is, try experimenting with different ones. Spend a week focusing on one love language at a time and see how she responds.

For example, in Week 1, focus on words of affirmation. Compliment her, express your appreciation, and see how she reacts. In Week 2, switch to acts of service—do things to help her out and see if that resonates with her. Continue this with each love language until you notice which one has the biggest impact.

This process might take some time, but it's worth it. Once you figure out her love language, you'll be able to communicate your love in a way that truly connects with her.

Speaking Her Love Language

Alright, fellas, now that you've identified your wife's love language, it's time to start speaking it. This is where the magic happens—where you start to see your efforts pay off in the form of a deeper connection, more appreciation, and a stronger bond. Let's go through each love language and talk about some practical ways you can start incorporating it into your relationship.

1. Words of Affirmation

If your wife's love language is words of affirmation, she feels most loved when you express your appreciation, encouragement, and love through words. This might come naturally to you, or it might be something you need to work on—but either way, it's worth the effort.

Here are some ways to speak her language:

- **Compliments:** Regularly tell your wife what you love about her. It could be anything from her appearance to her personality to something specific she did. For example, "You look beautiful today," or "I really appreciate how you always take care of the kids."

- **Appreciation:** Let her know that you notice and value what she does. If she's been working hard, acknowledge it. Say things like, "I'm so grateful for everything you do for our family," or "Thank you for always being there for me."

- **Encouragement:** If your wife is working towards a goal or going through a tough time, offer her words of encouragement. Remind her of her strengths, and let her know that you believe in her. For example, "I'm so proud of you for going after your dreams," or "You've got this—I believe in you."

- **Love Notes:** Sometimes, a simple note can make a big impact. Leave little love notes for her to find—on the bathroom mirror, in her purse, or on her pillow. It doesn't have to be anything elaborate; even a short "I love you" can mean a lot.

2. Acts of Service

If your wife's love language is acts of service, she feels most loved when you do things to help her out or make her life easier. This love language is all about action—showing your love by rolling up your sleeves and getting things done.

Here are some ways to speak her language:

- **Help with Chores:** Take on some of the household responsibilities, especially those that your wife usually handles. This could be anything from doing the dishes, cleaning the house, or taking care of the kids. The key is to do it without being asked and to do it with a positive attitude.

- **Run Errands:** If there are errands that your wife needs to run, offer to take care of them for her. This could be picking up groceries, dropping off dry cleaning, or making sure the car is serviced. These small acts of service can take a load off her shoulders.

- **Cook a Meal:** If you're not the one who usually cooks, surprise her by preparing a meal. It doesn't have to be gourmet—just the fact that you took the time and effort to cook for her will make her feel loved. Bonus points if it's one of her favorite dishes!

- **Support Her Goals:** If your wife has personal or professional goals, find ways to support her in achieving them. This could be as simple as helping her carve out time to work on her goals or taking on extra responsibilities so she can focus on what's important to her.

3. Receiving Gifts

If your wife's love language is receiving gifts, she feels most loved when you give her thoughtful gifts that show you've been thinking about her. This love language isn't about materialism—it's about the thought and effort behind the gift.

Here are some ways to speak her language:

- **Surprise Gifts:** Every now and then, surprise your wife with a small gift. It doesn't have to be anything extravagant—something as simple as her favorite chocolate, a book she's been wanting to read, or a bouquet of flowers can make her day.

- **Meaningful Tokens:** Give her something that has personal significance, like a piece of jewelry with her birthstone, a framed photo of a special memory, or a handwritten letter. These kinds of gifts show that you've put thought into what would make her happy.

- **Special Occasions:** Don't forget special occasions like birthdays, anniversaries, and holidays. Plan ahead and make sure you get her something that she'll love. It's not about the cost, but about making her feel cherished on these important days.

- **Just Because:** Sometimes, the best gifts are the ones that come out of nowhere—no special occasion, just because. It could be something small, like bringing her coffee in bed, or something more elaborate, like planning a surprise date night. These "just because" gifts show that you're thinking of her even when there's no reason to.

4. Quality Time

If your wife's love language is quality time, she feels most loved when you spend focused, undivided time with her. This love language is all about being present and making her feel like a priority.

Here are some ways to speak her language:

- **Unplug and Focus:** When you're spending time with your wife, make sure to eliminate distractions. Put your phone away, turn off the TV, and focus on her. This shows that you value your time together and that she has your full attention.

- **Plan Date Nights:** Regularly plan date nights where you can spend quality time together. It doesn't have to be anything elaborate—a simple dinner, a walk in the park, or a movie night at home can be just as special. The key is to make it a regular part of your routine.

- **Have Deep Conversations:** Make time for meaningful conversations where you can talk about your dreams, goals, and feelings. These conversations help you connect on a deeper level and show your wife that you care about what's going on in her life.

- **Share Activities:** Find activities that you both enjoy and do them together. Whether it's cooking, working out, or exploring new places, sharing these experiences can strengthen your bond and create lasting memories.

*5. Physical Touch

If your wife's love language is physical touch, she feels most loved when you're physically affectionate. This love language is all about the power of touch—whether it's holding hands, hugging, or more intimate forms of physical connection.

Here are some ways to speak her language:

- **Hold Hands:** When you're walking together, reach out and hold her hand. This simple gesture can make her feel connected to you and loved.

- **Hug and Kiss:** Make it a habit to hug and kiss your wife regularly—not just as a greeting or goodbye, but throughout the day. These small touches can make a big difference in how she feels.

- **Cuddle:** Spend time cuddling on the couch while watching a movie or just relaxing. Physical closeness without any distractions can make her feel safe and loved.

- **Intimacy:** Physical touch includes sexual intimacy, but it's important to approach it with sensitivity to her needs and desires. Make sure that intimacy is about connecting and showing love, rather than just fulfilling a physical need.

Challenges and Solutions

Now, I know what some of you might be thinking—what if my wife's love language is something I'm not naturally good at? What if speaking her love language feels awkward or uncomfortable?

First of all, it's okay to feel that way. We all have our strengths and weaknesses when it comes to expressing love, and it's natural to find some love languages easier than others. The important thing is to be willing to learn and grow. Here are some tips to help you overcome these challenges:

1. Practice Makes Perfect

If you're not naturally good at speaking your wife's love language, remember that practice makes perfect. The more you do it, the more comfortable it will become. Start small and build up over time. For example, if words of affirmation don't come easily to you, start by giving her one compliment a day. As you get more comfortable, you can start expressing your appreciation and encouragement more frequently.

2. Step Out of Your Comfort Zone

Growth happens when we step out of our comfort zones. If speaking your wife's love language feels awkward, that's okay—embrace the discomfort as part of the process. Remember, you're doing this because you love her and want to strengthen your relationship. The effort you put in will be worth it in the long run.

3. Communicate Openly

If you're struggling to speak your wife's love language, talk to her about it. Let her know that you're making an effort and that you want to learn how to love her in the way she needs. This open communication can help you both understand each other better and find ways to support each other in the process.

4. Be Patient

Learning to speak your wife's love language takes time and patience. Don't expect to get it perfect right away. Be patient with yourself and with your wife as you navigate this new territory. Celebrate the small victories and keep working at it.

Love in Action

Understanding and speaking your wife's love language is one of the most powerful ways you can show her that you love her. It's about meeting her where she is, in the way that resonates most deeply with her. When you speak her love language, you're not just saying "I love you"—you're showing it in a way that she truly feels.

But remember, this isn't just a one-time thing. Love languages are a lifelong journey. As your relationship evolves, so might her love language. Stay curious, stay attentive, and keep learning how to love her better every day.

So, fellas, let's make a commitment. Let's commit to understanding our wives' love languages and speaking them fluently. Let's commit to showing our love not just in words, but in actions that make our wives feel truly cherished. This is how we build strong, healthy, and lasting relationships. This is how we love deeply.

You've got this, my brothers. Let's go out there and love our wives in a way that speaks to their hearts.

The Importance of Emotional Vulnerability

Alright, fellas, let's talk about something real—something that most of us find pretty difficult to do: emotional vulnerability. I know, just hearing the word "vulnerability" might make some of you tense up or want to skip ahead to the next chapter, but hold up. This is important. It's crucial, in fact, if you want to have a deep, meaningful, and lasting relationship with your wife.

You see, being emotionally vulnerable isn't just about wearing your heart on your sleeve or sharing your deepest secrets with anyone who will listen. No, it's about something much deeper. It's about being honest with yourself and with the person you love. It's about creating a space in your marriage where both of you can be your true selves, without fear of judgment or rejection. When you open up emotionally, you build a foundation of trust, intimacy, and connection that can withstand the inevitable ups and downs of life.

Now, I'm not saying it's easy. Society often tells us as men that we need to be strong, stoic, and in control at all times. We're taught that showing emotion is a sign of weakness, that real men don't cry or admit when they're struggling. But let me tell you something—that's a load of garbage. True strength lies in the ability to be vulnerable, to let down your guard and share what's really going on inside you. And when you do that in your marriage, the rewards are immeasurable.

So, what we're gonna do is dive deep into what it means to be emotionally vulnerable with your wife. We'll talk about why it's so important, how to start opening up, and how to create a safe space for both of you to share your innermost thoughts and feelings. By the end of this chapter, you'll have a clearer understanding of how emotional vulnerability can transform your marriage, and you'll be equipped with practical tools to start making that change today.

Why Emotional Vulnerability Matters

First, let's break down why emotional vulnerability is so important in a marriage. Think of your relationship like a bridge. This bridge connects you and your wife, allowing you to share your lives, your experiences, and your love. But for that bridge to be strong, it needs to be built on trust, communication, and mutual understanding. Without vulnerability, that bridge is shaky at best. It might hold up for a while, but eventually, the weight of unspoken feelings, unresolved issues, and unexpressed emotions will cause it to collapse.

Emotional vulnerability is the foundation of intimacy. When you're open with your wife about your thoughts, feelings, fears, and dreams, you invite her to do the same. It creates a safe environment where both of you can be honest and authentic, without worrying about being judged or misunderstood. This kind of openness fosters trust, which is the cornerstone of any healthy relationship. When you trust each other enough to be vulnerable, you create a bond that's much stronger than any external force that might try to pull you apart.

But it's not just about strengthening your relationship—it's also about personal growth. When you allow yourself to be vulnerable, you give yourself permission to grow, to learn, and to evolve. You start to see that your emotions are not a sign of weakness, but a source of strength. You begin to understand that it's okay to not have all the answers, to ask for help, and to lean on your wife for support when you need it.

This process of opening up can also be incredibly healing. Many of us carry emotional wounds from the past—whether it's from childhood, past relationships, or societal pressures—that we've never fully dealt with. By being vulnerable, you allow yourself to confront these wounds, to talk about them, and to begin the process of healing. And when you do this alongside your wife, you're not only healing yourself, but you're also deepening the connection you share with her.

The Barriers to Emotional Vulnerability

Before we get into how to be more emotionally vulnerable, it's important to acknowledge the barriers that often prevent us from opening up. Understanding these barriers is the first step in overcoming them.

1. Fear of Rejection

One of the biggest barriers to emotional vulnerability is the fear of rejection. Many of us are afraid that if we open up about our true feelings, our fears, or our insecurities, we'll be rejected or judged. We worry that our wives might think less of us, or that they might not understand what we're going through. This fear can keep us locked up, preventing us from sharing what's really going on inside.

2. Shame

Shame is another powerful barrier. We often feel ashamed of our emotions, especially if they don't align with society's expectations of what a "real man" should be. We might feel ashamed of our fears, our failures, or our vulnerabilities, and as a result, we keep them hidden. But the problem with shame is that it thrives in secrecy. The more we keep our feelings buried, the more powerful that shame becomes.

3. Past Experiences

Many of us have been conditioned by past experiences to keep our emotions in check. Maybe you grew up in a household where emotions were not expressed, or perhaps you've been in relationships where your vulnerability was met with criticism or indifference. These past experiences can create a protective shell around us, making it difficult to open up, even with someone we trust.

4. Cultural Conditioning

Let's not forget the role of cultural conditioning. Society has long perpetuated the idea that men should be strong, silent, and in control. We're taught to "man up" and push through our emotions, to deal with our problems on our own. This cultural narrative can make it incredibly difficult to embrace vulnerability, as it's often seen as the opposite of what it means to be a "real man."

5. Lack of Practice

Finally, there's the simple fact that many of us have never really practiced being vulnerable. If you've spent most of your life keeping your emotions to yourself, it's no surprise that opening up feels foreign and uncomfortable. Vulnerability is a skill, and like any skill, it takes practice to develop.

Steps to Embracing Emotional Vulnerability

Now that we've identified some of the barriers to vulnerability, let's talk about how to start breaking them down. Embracing vulnerability is a journey, not a destination. It's something you'll need to work on continuously, but the rewards are well worth the effort.

1. Start with Self-Awareness

The first step to becoming more emotionally vulnerable is developing self-awareness. This means taking the time to reflect on your own emotions, thoughts, and behaviors. Ask yourself: What am I feeling right now? What am I afraid of? What's holding me back from opening up to my wife? By getting in touch with your own emotions, you'll start to understand where your resistance to vulnerability comes from.

Journaling can be a helpful tool in this process. Spend some time each day writing down your thoughts and feelings. Don't worry about being perfect—just let the words flow. Over time, you'll start to see patterns in your emotions and behaviors, which can give you valuable insights into what's really going on beneath the surface.

2. Challenge Negative Beliefs

Once you've identified the barriers to your vulnerability, it's time to start challenging them. If you're afraid of rejection, remind yourself that your wife loves you for who you are, not for some perfect version of yourself. If you're dealing with shame, remember that everyone has fears, insecurities, and vulnerabilities—there's no shame in being human.

It can also be helpful to question the societal norms that have conditioned you to suppress your emotions. Ask yourself: Who benefits from the idea that men should be strong and silent? Is it really serving you and your relationship to hold onto this belief? By challenging these negative beliefs, you'll start to loosen their grip on you.

3. Communicate Your Intentions

One of the most important steps in becoming more emotionally vulnerable is communicating your intentions to your wife. Let her know that you're working on opening up more, and that you want to create a space in your relationship where both of you can be vulnerable. This sets the stage for a deeper level of communication and helps your wife understand what you're trying to achieve.

You might say something like, "I've been thinking a lot about how I can be a better partner, and I realize that I haven't always been open with you about my feelings. I want to work on that, and I hope we can create a space where we can both share what's really going on inside us."

4. Take Small Steps

Vulnerability doesn't happen overnight, and it's important to start small. You don't need to dive into your deepest fears right away. Begin by sharing something that feels slightly uncomfortable, but not overwhelming. For example, you might share a recent experience that made you feel anxious or uncertain. As you get more comfortable with being vulnerable, you can start to share more personal and deeper emotions.

Remember, vulnerability is like a muscle—the more you use it, the stronger it becomes. Each time you open up, you're building your capacity for deeper connection and intimacy.

5. Listen and Validate

When your wife responds to your vulnerability, it's important to listen and validate her feelings as well. Vulnerability is a two-way street. By opening up, you're creating a space for her to do the same. When she shares her emotions with you, listen without judgment, and validate her experience.

You might say something like, "I really appreciate you sharing that with me. I can see how much that's been weighing on you, and I'm here for you." This kind of response reinforces the trust between you and shows your wife that her feelings are important to you.

6. Practice Patience

Becoming emotionally vulnerable is a process, and it's important to be patient with yourself and your wife as you navigate this new territory. There will be times when it feels difficult, uncomfortable, or even scary. That's okay—change is never easy. But with time and practice, you'll start to see the benefits of vulnerability in your relationship.

If you find yourself slipping back into old habits of emotional avoidance, don't beat yourself up. Acknowledge it, learn from it, and recommit to being open. Remember, this is a journey, and every step you take towards vulnerability is a step in the right direction.

7. Seek Support if Needed

If you're struggling with vulnerability and finding it difficult to open up, it might be helpful to seek support from a therapist or counselor. There's no shame in asking for help, especially when it comes to improving your relationship. A professional can provide guidance, tools, and strategies to help you develop emotional vulnerability and build a stronger connection with your wife.

The Benefits of Emotional Vulnerability

Now that we've talked about how to embrace vulnerability, let's look at some of the benefits you can expect to see in your marriage.

1. Deeper Connection

When you open up emotionally, you create a deeper connection with your wife. You move beyond surface-level conversations and start to explore the rich emotional landscape of your relationship. This deepening of connection can lead to a greater sense of intimacy, trust, and mutual understanding.

2. Increased Trust

Vulnerability builds trust. When you're open about your feelings, you're showing your wife that you trust her with your innermost thoughts and emotions. This act of trust encourages her to be vulnerable with you as well, creating a reciprocal relationship of trust and openness.

3. Greater Intimacy

Emotional vulnerability leads to greater intimacy in your marriage. When you're both open and honest with each other, you create a safe space where intimacy can flourish. This intimacy isn't just about physical closeness—it's about being emotionally connected and feeling truly understood by your partner.

4. Improved Communication

Vulnerability improves communication in your relationship. When you're open about your feelings, you're more likely to address issues before they become major problems. This proactive approach to communication can help prevent misunderstandings, conflicts, and resentment from building up over time.

5. Personal Growth

Finally, embracing vulnerability leads to personal growth. By confronting your fears, insecurities, and emotions, you're allowing yourself to grow and evolve as a person. This growth not only benefits your marriage but also contributes to your overall well-being and happiness.

The Power of Vulnerability

Alright, my brothers, we've covered a lot of ground in this chapter, and I hope you're starting to see just how powerful emotional vulnerability can be in your marriage. It's not about being weak or soft—it's about being real, honest, and authentic with yourself and your wife.

When you embrace vulnerability, you're making a commitment to deepen your connection, build trust, and create a relationship that's built on a foundation of mutual understanding and respect. It's not always easy, but it's worth it.

So I challenge you to take that first step towards vulnerability. Start small, be patient with yourself, and remember that this is a journey. As you open up and allow yourself to be vulnerable, you'll start to see the incredible impact it has on your marriage and your life.

You've got this. Now go out there and love your wife in a way that's real, deep, and authentic. Let her see the true you, and watch as your relationship transforms in ways you never thought possible.

Showing Up Every Day

Hey, fellas. Today, we're diving into something fundamental, something that can make or break your marriage over time: consistency. I'm talking about showing up every single day for your wife, not just when it's convenient or when it suits you, but every day. It's about being there in the big moments and, more importantly, in the small, seemingly insignificant moments that truly define a relationship.

You know, love isn't just a grand gesture or a once-in-a-while romantic getaway. While those things are great, they're not the glue that holds your marriage together. What really matters, what really counts, is the way you show up daily. It's the consistent effort, the small acts of kindness, and the steady presence that let your wife know she's always on your mind. These actions build trust, security, and deep love over time.

Now, I know life gets busy. Work, kids, responsibilities—they all demand our attention. But here's the thing: Your marriage, your relationship with your wife, should be at the top of that list. Consistency in showing up isn't just about time; it's about prioritization and making sure that your wife knows she's a priority in your life. When you show up consistently, you're telling her, "You matter to me, every single day." And that, my friends, is what builds a solid, unshakeable marriage.

So, we're going to explore what it means to show up every day, why it's so important, and how you can do it in ways that resonate with your wife. We're going to break it down into practical steps so you can start implementing this immediately, and watch as it transforms your relationship.

The Power of Consistency in Love

Let's start with the why. Why is consistency so powerful in a relationship? Imagine this: You're building a house. If you lay a brick one day, then skip a few days, maybe lay another brick a week later, and so on—how long is it going to take to build that house? Will it ever really be solid? Probably not. Now imagine you lay a brick every single day. No matter what happens, you're out there, adding to the structure. Over time, you'll have a sturdy, reliable house, built on a foundation of consistent effort.

Your marriage is that house. Every small, consistent action you take is like laying a brick in the foundation of your relationship. These actions might seem insignificant on their own, but over time, they build something strong, something that can withstand the storms of life.

Consistency breeds trust. When you show up every day, your wife knows she can rely on you. She doesn't have to wonder if you're going to be there when she needs you because you've proven, time and time again, that you are. This creates a sense of security, which is crucial in any marriage. Your consistent actions tell her, "I'm here for you. I'm not going anywhere."

And it's not just about trust; it's about love, too. Consistency is how you show your wife that she's always on your mind. It's how you communicate that she matters, that you're thinking about her even in the midst of life's chaos. It's the morning kiss, the midday text, the help with chores, the little things that say, "I love you," without needing to say the words.

Showing Up in the Small Moments

We often think that love is all about the big gestures—the surprise vacation, the fancy dinner, the expensive gift. But let me tell you something: it's the small moments that really count. The small, everyday actions that show you're there, that you're present, that you care.

1. The Morning Kiss

One of the simplest yet most powerful ways to show up every day is to start each morning with a kiss. Now, this might sound trivial, but it's not. That morning kiss is a ritual, a small act that says, "I'm glad to wake up next to you." It sets the tone for the day and reinforces your connection before you both go off into your separate worlds.

Think about it: How often do we rush through our mornings, barely saying goodbye as we head out the door? What if you took just a few seconds to stop, look her in the eyes, and give her a kiss? It's a small act, but it has a big impact. It's a way to show up right from the start of the day.

2. Thoughtful Texts and Check-Ins

Life gets busy, and sometimes, it's easy to get caught up in our own worlds. But a quick text in the middle of the day can be a game-changer. Something as simple as, "Thinking of you," or "How's your day going?" shows that she's on your mind. It doesn't have to be anything elaborate. Just a little reminder that you're there, that you're thinking about her, can mean the world.

These small check-ins keep the connection alive throughout the day. They break up the routine and remind her that she's not forgotten, that she's a priority even in the middle of everything else you have going on.

3. Helping Out with Chores

Now, this one might not sound romantic, but trust me, it's huge. Helping out with chores is one of the most practical ways to show up every day. Whether it's doing the dishes, taking out the trash, or folding the laundry—these small acts of service show that you're in this together.

When you step up and take on some of the household responsibilities, you're saying, "I see you, and I appreciate everything you do." You're also showing that you're willing to share the load, that you're a partner in every sense of the word. This kind of consistency goes a long way in making your wife feel supported and valued.

4. Being Present

Being present is about more than just being physically there—it's about being mentally and emotionally available. When you're with your wife, are you really with her? Are you listening, engaging, and connecting? Or are you distracted, thinking about work, or scrolling through your phone?

One of the most consistent ways to show up for your wife is to be fully present when you're together. This means putting down the phone, turning off the TV, and really focusing on her. Listen to what she's saying, engage in the conversation, and make her feel heard. Being present might sound simple, but in today's world, it's something we have to be intentional about.

5. Small Gestures of Affection

Sometimes, it's the little things that make the biggest difference. A gentle touch on the arm as you walk by, a hug when she least expects it, a cup of coffee waiting for her in the morning—these small gestures of affection are powerful ways to show up every day.

These gestures don't require a lot of time or effort, but they do require thoughtfulness. They show that you're thinking about her, that you're tuned in to her needs and desires. Over time, these small acts of affection build up and create a strong, loving connection.

Building a Routine of Consistency

Alright, so we've talked about the small moments and why they matter. But how do you turn these actions into a routine, into something that you do consistently every day? Let's break it down into actionable steps.

1. Start with a Daily Ritual

A daily ritual is something you commit to doing every single day, no matter what. It's a small, consistent action that becomes a habit over time. This could be something as simple as the morning kiss we talked about earlier. By making this a daily ritual, you're starting each day with a positive, loving action that reinforces your connection.

Another idea for a daily ritual could be a nightly check-in. Before you go to bed, take a few minutes to ask your wife how her day was, what's on her mind, and how she's feeling. This creates a routine of communication and connection that helps you stay in tune with each other.

2. Set Reminders

Let's be real—life gets busy, and it's easy to forget even the simplest things. Setting reminders on your phone can be a helpful way to stay consistent. Whether it's a reminder to send a quick text in the middle of the day or to pick up flowers on your way home, these little prompts can help you stay on track.

Remember, it's not about the reminders themselves; it's about the intention behind them. You're setting these reminders because you want to show up for your wife consistently, and sometimes, we all need a little nudge to stay on course.

3. Make Time for Quality Moments

Quality time doesn't just happen—you have to make time for it. This means being intentional about carving out time in your schedule to spend with your wife. Whether it's a weekly date night, a walk after dinner, or simply sitting down together for a cup of coffee in the morning, these moments of quality time are essential.

The key here is consistency. It's not about how much time you spend together, but how often you make that time. Regular, quality moments of connection build a strong foundation for your relationship.

4. Be Mindful of Her Needs

Consistency isn't just about doing the same thing every day; it's about being mindful of your wife's needs and responding to them regularly. This requires paying attention, listening, and being in tune with what she needs from you. Maybe she needs a little extra support during a stressful week, or maybe she's craving some alone time—being mindful and responsive to her needs is a powerful way to show up consistently.

Being consistent also means being reliable. If you say you're going to do something, follow through. If she's counting on you to handle something, make sure it gets done. This kind of reliability builds trust and shows her that she can depend on you, day in and day out.

5. Practice Gratitude

Gratitude is a powerful force in any relationship. Make it a habit to express gratitude to your wife every day. This could be a simple "thank you" for something she's done or a heartfelt expression of appreciation for who she is and what she brings to your life.

When you consistently express gratitude, you're focusing on the positive aspects of your relationship. You're reinforcing the good and making sure your wife knows that she's valued and appreciated. Over time, this practice of gratitude strengthens your bond and creates a positive, loving environment in your marriage.

The Challenges of Consistency

Now, let's be real for a minute—showing up every day isn't always easy. There will be days when you're tired, stressed, or just not in the mood. Life happens, and it can be challenging to stay consistent, especially when you're dealing with your own pressures and responsibilities.

But here's the thing: consistency is about commitment. It's about making a decision to show up every day, no matter what. Even on the hard days, even when it's inconvenient, you're choosing to prioritize your marriage and your wife.

It's okay if you don't get it right all the time. We're all human, and we all have our off days. What's important is that you don't give up. If you miss a day, don't beat yourself up—just get back on track and keep moving forward.

Consistency is also about being flexible. Life is unpredictable, and sometimes, your routine might need to change. Maybe you have to adjust your daily ritual because of a new work schedule or because you're traveling. That's okay—what matters is that you stay committed to showing up in whatever way you can, even if it looks a little different from day to day.

The Long-Term Impact of Consistency

Alright, let's talk about the long game. What happens when you consistently show up for your wife every day? Over time, these small, consistent actions create a relationship that's strong, resilient, and deeply connected.

When you show up every day, you're building a marriage that can withstand the ups and downs of life. You're creating a foundation of trust, love, and reliability that will carry you through the challenges and the joys. This kind of relationship doesn't just happen—it's built brick by brick, day by day, through consistent effort.

Your wife will feel valued, loved, and secure, knowing that you're always there for her. She'll know that she can count on you, not just in the big moments, but in the small, everyday moments that make up your life together.

And let's not forget about the impact on you. When you show up consistently, you're also showing up for yourself. You're becoming the kind of partner who is reliable, loving, and present. This kind of consistency helps you grow as a person and deepens your understanding of what it means to love and be loved.

The Power of Showing Up Every Day

Fellas, we've covered a lot in this chapter, and I hope you're starting to see just how powerful consistency can be in your marriage. It's not about grand gestures or occasional efforts—it's about the small, everyday actions that show your wife that she's always on your mind.

When you show up every day, you're building a marriage that's strong, resilient, and deeply connected. You're creating a foundation of trust, love, and reliability that will carry you through the challenges and joys of life.

So, I challenge you to start showing up every day, in the small moments and the big ones. Start with a daily ritual, be present, help out, and express gratitude. Make consistency a priority in your marriage, and watch as it transforms your relationship in ways you never thought possible.

You've got this. Show up for your wife, show up for your marriage, and show up for yourself. Because when you do, you're not just building a strong relationship—you're building a life together, one that's filled with love, connection, and lasting happiness.

The Art of Appreciation

Alright, fellas, let's talk about something that often gets lost in the hustle and bustle of daily life: appreciation. Now, I know that word might sound simple, almost too simple, but let me tell you, it's one of the most powerful tools you have in your relationship toolkit. The art of appreciation is about more than just saying "thank you" every now and then. It's about truly recognizing, valuing, and celebrating your wife for who she is and everything she does—big or small.

When was the last time you truly showed your wife how much you appreciate her? I'm not talking about a quick, offhand comment, but a genuine expression of gratitude for who she is and what she brings to your life. If it's been a while, you're not alone. Life has a way of pulling us in a million different directions, and sometimes we forget to slow down and really see the people we love the most. But here's the thing—appreciation is like oxygen for your marriage. Without it, things can start to suffocate.

We're going to dig deep into what it means to appreciate your wife, why it's so crucial for a healthy relationship, and how you can make it a regular part of your daily life. We're going to go beyond the basics and explore how you can turn appreciation into an art form, something that comes naturally and consistently. Because when your wife feels truly appreciated, she feels valued, respected, and loved—and that, my friends, is the foundation of a strong, lasting marriage.

The Power of Genuine Appreciation

Let's start by talking about why appreciation matters so much. When you consistently show your wife that you appreciate her, you're reinforcing her sense of worth and importance in your life. You're telling her, "I see you. I value you. I don't take you for granted." And that's a message every person needs to hear, especially from the one they love most.

Appreciation builds connection. It bridges the gap between you and your wife, reminding both of you why you fell in love in the first place. It keeps the positive energy flowing and helps to counteract the inevitable challenges and stresses that come with life. When appreciation is present in your marriage, it acts like a buffer against negativity. It's hard to stay upset with someone who just made you feel truly valued, right?

But here's the thing—appreciation has to be genuine. It can't be something you do out of obligation or because you think it's what you're supposed to do. Your wife will pick up on that immediately, and it'll lose its impact. Genuine appreciation comes from a place of deep gratitude and recognition of the unique qualities and contributions your wife brings to your life.

When you genuinely appreciate your wife, you're acknowledging her worth. You're letting her know that she's seen, heard, and valued for exactly who she is. This kind of validation is powerful. It strengthens her confidence, nurtures her sense of self, and deepens the emotional connection between you. It's about making her feel special and irreplaceable, not just as a wife, but as a person.

Recognizing the Little Things

Now, let's talk about what appreciation actually looks like in action. Often, we think of appreciation in terms of the big things—thanking your wife for throwing a great dinner party, or for the way she takes care of the kids. And while those things are definitely worth appreciating, it's the little things that often go unnoticed that can make the biggest difference.

Think about all the small, everyday things your wife does that you might take for granted. Maybe she always remembers to buy your favorite snacks, or she makes sure the house feels warm and welcoming when you get home from work. Maybe she listens patiently when you've had a tough day, or she sends you a text just to say she's thinking of you. These are the things that can easily blend into the background of daily life, but they're also the things that make life sweeter, easier, and more connected.

Start by paying attention to these little things. Make it a point to notice them. The next time your wife does something small but meaningful, take a moment to acknowledge it. It could be something as simple as saying, "I really appreciate how you always make sure we have everything we need," or "It means a lot to me that you always make time to listen when I'm stressed."

When you start to notice and appreciate the little things, something amazing happens. Your wife feels seen and valued in a way that goes beyond the obvious. She feels like you truly understand and recognize her efforts, and that kind of recognition is incredibly powerful. It shows that you're paying attention, that you care about the details of her life and the little ways she contributes to your shared life together.

Expressing Appreciation Regularly

Alright, so you've started to notice the little things—now what? How do you turn that recognition into a regular practice of appreciation? It's all about consistency, fellas. Appreciation isn't a one-time thing; it's something you need to express regularly, in different ways, to keep your relationship strong and healthy.

Here are a few strategies to help you express appreciation consistently:

1. Verbal Acknowledgment

This is the most straightforward way to express appreciation, but it's also one of the most effective. Make it a habit to verbally acknowledge the things your wife does that you appreciate. It could be something as simple as, "Thank you for making dinner tonight—it was delicious," or "I really appreciate how you handled that situation with the kids today."

Don't wait for big moments to express your appreciation. Instead, try to incorporate it into your daily interactions. When you make verbal acknowledgment a regular part of your communication, it becomes a natural way of showing love and respect.

2. Written Notes and Messages

Sometimes, written words can have an even greater impact than spoken ones. A handwritten note or a thoughtful text can be a powerful way to express your appreciation. Leave a note on her pillow, in her bag, or somewhere she'll find it unexpectedly. It doesn't have to be long or elaborate—just a few words to let her know you're thinking of her and appreciating what she does.

You might write something like, "I noticed how hard you've been working lately, and I just want to say thank you. I appreciate everything you do for our family." Or maybe, "Just wanted to let you know how much I love and appreciate you. You make my life better every day."

The key is to make it personal and specific. A generic "thank you" is nice, but a note that speaks directly to her efforts or qualities will resonate much more deeply.

3. Acts of Service

Actions often speak louder than words. One of the best ways to show appreciation is through acts of service. This could mean taking on a task that she usually handles, like cooking dinner, doing the laundry, or taking the kids out for the afternoon so she can have some time to herself.

When you step in to help out, you're not just taking something off her plate—you're showing that you recognize and value the effort she puts into those tasks. You're saying, "I see how hard you work, and I want to support you."

These acts of service don't have to be grand gestures. Sometimes, the smallest actions, like making her a cup of coffee in the morning or filling up her car with gas, can have the biggest impact. It's about being thoughtful and considerate, showing her that you're aware of her needs and willing to help meet them.

4. Quality Time

Another powerful way to express appreciation is through quality time. When you set aside time to be fully present with your wife, you're showing her that she's a priority in your life. This could be something as simple as sitting down to have a conversation without distractions, going for a walk together, or planning a date night.

Quality time is about more than just being physically present—it's about being mentally and emotionally engaged. It's about listening, sharing, and connecting. When you give your wife your undivided attention, you're saying, "I value our relationship, and I appreciate the time we spend together."

Making Appreciation a Habit

Now that we've talked about different ways to express appreciation, let's focus on how to make it a habit. Like anything else in life, showing appreciation takes practice and intention. But the more you do it, the more natural it becomes.

Here are some tips to help you build a habit of appreciation:

1. Reflect on Gratitude Daily

One of the easiest ways to build a habit of appreciation is to incorporate it into your daily routine. Take a few minutes each day to reflect on what you're grateful for in your marriage. This could be something you do in the morning, as part of your daily meditation or journaling practice, or something you do in the evening, as you wind down before bed.

Ask yourself: What did my wife do today that I'm grateful for? How did she make my day better? What qualities or actions do I appreciate in her? By regularly reflecting on these questions, you'll start to notice more and more things to appreciate, and expressing that appreciation will become second nature.

2. Start a Gratitude Journal

If you want to take your daily reflections a step further, consider starting a gratitude journal. Each day, write down at least one thing you appreciate about your wife. It could be something specific she did that day, or it could be a general quality or trait that you value in her.

Over time, this practice will help you become more attuned to the positive aspects of your relationship. It will also give you a tangible record of your gratitude, something you can look back on to remind yourself of all the reasons you love and appreciate your wife.

3. Share Your Gratitude Regularly

Once you've made a habit of reflecting on gratitude, the next step is to share it with your wife. Make it a point to regularly express your appreciation, whether through words, notes, acts of service, or quality time. The more you practice, the more natural it will become.

Remember, appreciation doesn't have to be a big, grand gesture. Sometimes, the simplest expressions can have the most profound impact. The key is to be consistent and genuine. When you make appreciation a regular part of your relationship, you're creating a positive, loving environment that strengthens your connection and deepens your bond.

4. Celebrate Her Uniqueness

One of the most meaningful ways to appreciate your wife is to celebrate her uniqueness. Every person has qualities that make them special, and it's important to recognize and celebrate those qualities in your wife. Whether it's her sense of humor, her creativity, her kindness, or her strength, let her know that you see and value what makes her unique.

Take time to reflect on the qualities that drew you to your wife in the first place. What do you love most about her? What makes her different from anyone else you've ever met? Share these reflections with her, and let her know how much you appreciate the unique person she is.

The Ripple Effect of Appreciation

Now that we've explored the art of appreciation, let's talk about the ripple effect it can have on your marriage. When you consistently express appreciation, you're not just making your wife feel good—you're creating a positive cycle that benefits your entire relationship.

Here's how it works: When your wife feels appreciated, she's more likely to feel happy, fulfilled, and connected in the relationship. This, in turn, makes her more likely to express appreciation for you, creating a cycle of positive reinforcement. Over time, this cycle builds a strong foundation of mutual respect, love, and gratitude.

But the ripple effect doesn't stop there. When appreciation becomes a regular part of your marriage, it can also have a positive impact on other areas of your life. You'll likely find that you're more patient, more understanding, and more empathetic in your interactions with your wife. You may also find that your overall mood improves, as you focus more on the positive aspects of your relationship and less on the negatives.

In addition, the practice of appreciation can extend beyond your marriage. As you become more attuned to the positive aspects of your wife and your relationship, you may find that you start to notice and appreciate the good in other areas of your life as well. This could be in your work, your friendships, or your interactions with others. The more you practice appreciation, the more it becomes a mindset, one that brings positivity and gratitude into every aspect of your life.

The Art of Appreciation in Your Marriage

Fellas, we've covered a lot of ground in this chapter, and I hope you're starting to see just how powerful the art of appreciation can be in your marriage. It's not about grand gestures or over-the-top expressions of gratitude—it's about consistently and genuinely recognizing and celebrating your wife for who she is and everything she does.

When you make appreciation a regular part of your relationship, you're building a strong foundation of love, respect, and gratitude. You're creating a positive cycle that benefits both you and your wife, deepening your connection and strengthening your bond. And as you practice appreciation, you'll likely find that it has a ripple effect, bringing positivity and gratitude into every area of your life.

So, I challenge you to start practicing the art of appreciation today. Start by noticing the little things your wife does, and make it a habit to express your gratitude regularly. Celebrate her uniqueness, and let her know just how much you value and appreciate her. When you do, you'll be creating a marriage that's filled with love, connection, and lasting happiness.

You've got this. Appreciate your wife, appreciate your marriage, and appreciate the life you're building together. Because when you do, you're not just strengthening your relationship—you're creating a life that's rich with love, gratitude, and joy.

Rekindling the Romance

Alright, my brothers, let's get real for a minute. We all know that romance isn't just for the honeymoon phase, right? But here's the thing—life happens. You get busy, you get comfortable, and before you know it, that spark you had when you first got together starts to flicker a little. Maybe you think, "We've been together for years, she knows I love her," and you're right—she probably does. But knowing she's loved and feeling that passion, that excitement, that *romance*—those are two different things. And keeping that romance alive, well, that's where the magic happens.

In this chapter, we're going to talk about how to rekindle the romance in your marriage, no matter how long you've been together. This isn't just about grand gestures or trying to recreate the early days of your relationship. It's about understanding what romance really is, why it's so important, and how you can weave it into the fabric of your daily life with your wife. Trust me, romance isn't just a "nice-to-have"—it's essential to keeping your marriage strong, connected, and full of that fire you both felt when you first fell in love.

Let's dive in and explore how you can keep that spark alive, remind your wife that she's still the one who makes your heart race, and show her that the romance in your relationship is here to stay.

What Romance Really Means

First things first, let's redefine what romance is all about. A lot of people think romance is all about flowers, candlelit dinners, and sweeping gestures, and while those things can be romantic, they're not the whole story. Romance is about creating moments that make your wife feel special, cherished, and loved. It's about putting in the effort to show her that she still lights up your world, no matter how many years you've been together.

Romance isn't about trying to impress her or win her over—it's about maintaining that emotional connection that brought you together in the first place. It's about keeping the excitement alive and reminding each other that your love is still growing, still evolving, and still worth celebrating. When you bring romance into your relationship, you're saying, "I still see you, I still adore you, and I'm still crazy about you."

But here's the key—romance doesn't have to be grand or expensive. It can be found in the small, thoughtful gestures that show you're thinking about her, that you value her, and that you're still committed to making her feel loved. So let's break down some practical ways to rekindle the romance and keep it alive, day in and day out.

Planning Spontaneous Dates

One of the easiest ways to keep the romance alive is by planning spontaneous dates. Now, I know what you might be thinking—"I've got a busy schedule, kids, work, responsibilities—how am I supposed to find time for spontaneous dates?" But here's the thing—romance thrives on spontaneity. It doesn't have to be a grand event that requires weeks of planning. In fact, some of the most romantic moments happen when they're least expected.

Start by thinking about the kinds of dates you both enjoyed when you first started dating. Was it going out for a late-night dessert, taking a walk in the park, or maybe even just sitting on the couch watching your favorite show? Whatever it was, find a way to bring that same energy back into your relationship. The key is to surprise her with something that feels special and out of the ordinary, something that breaks the routine and reminds her of the excitement you felt when you first started falling in love.

For example, you might come home from work and say, "Get ready, we're going out tonight." Don't tell her where you're going—keep it a surprise. Maybe it's dinner at that little spot you both love, or maybe it's something new that you've been meaning to try. The destination isn't as important as the fact that you're taking the initiative to plan something special, just for the two of you.

If you're short on time or can't get away for a full evening, you can still create spontaneous moments at home. How about a surprise candlelit dinner in your living room? Cook her favorite meal, light some candles, and put on some music that means something to both of you. Or, if you're not much of a cook, order takeout from her favorite restaurant and make it an impromptu date night. The point is to do something out of the ordinary that makes her feel special and loved.

The Power of Love Notes

Let's talk about one of the simplest, yet most powerful ways to keep the romance alive—love notes. Now, I know we're all living in the age of texts and emails, but there's something timeless about a handwritten note that just can't be replaced. Love notes are a way to express your feelings in a way that's personal, thoughtful, and lasting. They're a small gesture that can have a huge impact.

You don't have to be a poet to write a meaningful love note. It doesn't have to be long or elaborate—just a few heartfelt words can go a long way. The key is to be genuine and to speak from the heart. Think about what you love most about your wife, what you appreciate about her, or even just a simple message to let her know you're thinking of her.

For example, you might write something like, "Just wanted to remind you how much I love you and how grateful I am to have you in my life." Or, "Every day with you is a blessing—I'm so lucky to be your husband." It doesn't have to be anything fancy—just a few words to let her know she's on your mind and in your heart.

And don't just leave these notes for special occasions—make it a regular habit. Slip a note into her purse before she heads out for the day, leave one on her pillow, or stick one on the bathroom mirror for her to find in the morning. These little surprises will brighten her day and remind her that your love is still strong, still passionate, and still full of romance.

Creating New Shared Experiences

Another key to rekindling the romance is to create new shared experiences. When you're caught up in the day-to-day routine, it's easy to fall into a pattern where every day feels the same. And while routines can be comforting, they can also make it easy to take each other for granted. One of the best ways to break out of that routine and reignite the spark is to try new things together.

Think about something you've always wanted to do as a couple but haven't gotten around to yet. Maybe it's taking a cooking class together, going on a weekend getaway, or trying a new hobby like dancing, painting, or hiking. Whatever it is, the goal is to do something that's out of the ordinary and that allows you to connect in a new way.

New experiences create excitement and give you something to look forward to and bond over. They also remind you that there's always more to explore in your relationship, no matter how long you've been together. When you're trying something new, you're both stepping out of your comfort zones and discovering new sides of each other, which can reignite that sense of curiosity and passion that you felt when you first started dating.

And remember, it's not just about the big experiences—it's about finding joy in the small, everyday moments too. Even something as simple as trying a new recipe together, exploring a different part of your city, or starting a new tradition can bring fresh energy into your relationship and help keep the romance alive.

Prioritizing Physical Intimacy

Let's be real—physical intimacy is a big part of keeping the romance alive. But I'm not just talking about sex, although that's certainly important. I'm talking about all the little ways you can stay physically connected with your wife on a daily basis. Touch is a powerful way to express love, and it's something that can easily get lost in the busyness of life.

Start by making an effort to be more physically affectionate with your wife. Hold her hand when you're walking together, give her a hug when you see her after a long day, or just touch her arm when you're sitting next to each other. These small gestures can make a big difference in how connected you feel to each other.

Don't underestimate the power of a goodnight kiss, a cuddle on the couch, or a playful touch when you're cooking dinner together. These moments of physical connection help to keep the romance alive and remind both of you that your relationship is built on a foundation of love, affection, and intimacy.

And yes, making time for sexual intimacy is important too. It's easy to let this aspect of your relationship slide when you're busy, tired, or stressed, but it's essential to keeping the spark alive. Make it a priority to connect with your wife in this way, even if it means scheduling time for it. I know that might not sound romantic, but sometimes life requires a little planning. The key is to make it a regular part of your relationship, not something that only happens when everything else is perfect.

Remember, physical intimacy is about more than just the act itself—it's about the connection, the closeness, and the love that you share with your wife. When you prioritize physical intimacy, you're nurturing the romantic side of your relationship and keeping that spark alive.

Keeping the Element of Surprise

One of the most exciting aspects of romance is the element of surprise. When you surprise your wife with something unexpected, you're breaking the routine and adding a little excitement to your relationship. Surprises show that you're thinking about her and that you're willing to put in the effort to keep things fresh and exciting.

Surprises don't have to be big or expensive—they just need to be thoughtful. Maybe it's bringing home her favorite treat after a long day, planning a surprise date night, or even just taking care of a task she's been dreading. The point is to do something that makes her feel special and appreciated, something that shows her you're still thinking about her and that you're still invested in your relationship.

Another idea is to surprise her with something that's just for her—something that shows you know and appreciate her as an individual. Maybe it's a book by her favorite author, a new outfit in her favorite color, or even just a handwritten note telling her how much you love her. These little surprises can go a long way in keeping the romance alive and showing your wife that you're still crazy about her.

Keeping the Romance Alive Every Day

Now that we've talked about some specific ways to rekindle the romance, let's talk about how you can keep that romance alive every single day. The truth is, romance isn't just about the big gestures or the special occasions—it's about the small, everyday actions that show your wife she's loved and cherished.

One of the best ways to do this is by being present and engaged in your relationship. When you're with your wife, be fully present—put away your phone, make eye contact, and really listen to what she's saying. Show her that you value your time together and that you're committed to making her feel loved and appreciated.

Another way to keep the romance alive is by being thoughtful and considerate in your everyday actions. This could mean doing something as simple as making her morning coffee, taking care of a task she's been dreading, or just giving her a compliment that makes her feel good about herself. The key is to find small ways to show her that you're thinking about her and that you're still invested in making her happy.

And don't forget to keep things light and fun. Laughter is a big part of romance, and it's something that can easily get lost in the stress of everyday life. Find ways to make each other laugh, whether it's through an inside joke, a playful tease, or just being silly together. Laughter helps to keep the romance alive by reminding you both that your relationship is built on love, joy, and connection.

The Power of Romance in Your Marriage

Fellas, I want to leave you with this thought—romance isn't just a phase, it's a way of life. It's about making the choice, every day, to keep that spark alive in your relationship. It's about being thoughtful, intentional, and committed to showing your wife that she's still the one who makes your heart race.

When you make romance a priority, you're not just creating moments of love and connection—you're building a strong, passionate, and lasting relationship. You're showing your wife that your love is still growing, still evolving, and still worth celebrating. And you're creating a marriage that's filled with joy, excitement, and that beautiful, undeniable spark.

So, I challenge you to start rekindling the romance in your marriage today. Plan that spontaneous date, write that love note, and find ways to create new shared experiences with your wife. Keep the element of surprise alive, prioritize physical intimacy, and be present and engaged in your relationship every single day.

You've got this, my brothers. Keep that romance alive, and watch your marriage thrive. Because when you do, you're not just keeping the spark alive—you're creating a love story that's as exciting, passionate, and beautiful as the day you first fell in love. And that, my friends, is what makes a marriage truly special.

Supporting Her Dreams

Alright, fellas, let's talk about something that's near and dear to my heart—supporting your wife's dreams. Now, I know we all have our own goals and ambitions, and it's easy to get caught up in the hustle of chasing after what we want. But let me tell you something that's going to take your relationship to the next level: When you truly support your wife's dreams, you're not just helping her achieve her goals—you're strengthening your marriage, deepening your connection, and showing her that you're in this together, no matter what.

See, your wife's dreams and aspirations are just as important as yours. Her goals, whether they're big or small, professional or personal, are a huge part of who she is. And when you show up as her biggest cheerleader, you're letting her know that you see her, that you value what she wants out of life, and that you're committed to helping her get there. It's about being her partner in the truest sense of the word—someone who's got her back, who believes in her, and who's ready to put in the work to see her thrive.

But let's be real—supporting her dreams isn't just about saying "I'm proud of you" or giving her a pat on the back. It's about understanding what she really wants, being there for her through the ups and downs, and actively participating in her journey. It's about lifting her up when she's feeling discouraged, celebrating her victories, and helping her navigate the challenges along the way.

In this chapter, we're going to dive deep into what it really means to support your wife's dreams. We're going to talk about how you can be her biggest advocate, how you can help her set and achieve her goals, and how you can show her, day in and day out, that you're in this together. So let's get into it, my brothers—because when you support her dreams, you're not just helping her reach her potential—you're creating a marriage that's built on love, respect, and a shared vision for the future.

Understanding Her Dreams

The first step in supporting your wife's dreams is understanding what those dreams actually are. This might sound obvious, but you'd be surprised how many people go through life not really knowing what their partner's true passions and goals are. If you want to be the best support system for your wife, you've got to start by really understanding what she wants out of life.

Now, I'm not just talking about the surface-level stuff. Sure, you might know that she wants to advance in her career or maybe start a business someday, but do you really know *why* those things are important to her? Do you know what drives her, what she's passionate about, what lights her up inside? Understanding her dreams means digging deeper and having those real, honest conversations about what she wants for herself and for your life together.

Start by asking her about her goals and dreams. And when you do, really listen—don't just nod along or think about what you're going to say next. Ask open-ended questions like, "What's something you've always wanted to do but haven't had the chance to?" or "What are you most passionate about in your work or your hobbies?" The goal here is to understand her dreams on a deeper level, to see the full picture of what she wants to achieve, and to learn what's most important to her.

And don't assume that you already know everything. People's dreams evolve over time, and what she wanted five years ago might not be what she wants now. So make it a point to have these conversations regularly. Check in with her about her goals and how they might be changing. Show her that you're invested in her dreams, not just as her partner, but as someone who genuinely cares about her happiness and fulfillment.

Being Her Biggest Cheerleader

Once you understand what your wife's dreams are, the next step is to become her biggest cheerleader. And I'm not talking about just being supportive in theory—I'm talking about actively and consistently showing up for her, encouraging her, and celebrating her progress every step of the way.

Being a cheerleader means believing in her, even when she might have doubts about herself. It means reminding her of her strengths, her talents, and her potential, especially when she's feeling discouraged or overwhelmed. It's about being that voice of positivity and encouragement that keeps her going when things get tough.

But it's also about celebrating her wins, big and small. When she achieves a goal, whether it's landing a new client at work, finishing a project she's been working on, or even just making progress toward a long-term dream, take the time to celebrate it with her. Acknowledge her hard work, tell her how proud you are, and make a big deal out of it. These celebrations don't have to be elaborate—a heartfelt compliment, a special dinner, or even just a high-five can go a long way in showing her that you're in her corner, cheering her on.

And don't forget to be there for the setbacks, too. Not every step toward her dreams is going to be smooth sailing, and there will be times when she feels frustrated or disappointed. During those times, your role as her cheerleader is even more important. Be there to listen, to offer comfort, and to remind her that setbacks are just part of the journey. Encourage her to keep going, to learn from the challenges, and to keep her eyes on the bigger picture.

Making Space for Her Dreams

Supporting your wife's dreams also means making space for them in your life together. This might mean adjusting your schedule, sharing responsibilities differently, or making sacrifices to ensure she has the time and energy to pursue her goals. It's about recognizing that her dreams are just as important as yours and that they deserve the time, attention, and resources needed to come to fruition.

Start by looking at your daily routines and responsibilities. Are there ways you can adjust things to give her more time to focus on her goals? For example, if she's working on a big project or trying to build a side business, maybe you take on more of the household chores during that time, or you arrange for childcare so she can have uninterrupted time to work. It's about being proactive and finding ways to lighten her load so she can dedicate more of herself to what she's passionate about.

But it's not just about the practical side of things—it's also about emotional support. Pursuing a dream can be mentally and emotionally draining, especially when you're balancing it with other responsibilities. Be there to offer a listening ear, to provide encouragement, and to remind her that it's okay to take time for herself and her goals. Make it clear that her dreams are a priority in your relationship and that you're willing to do what it takes to help her succeed.

Helping Her Set and Achieve Goals

Supporting your wife's dreams isn't just about cheering her on from the sidelines—it's about actively helping her set and achieve her goals. This means being involved in the process, offering your skills and resources, and helping her stay on track toward her objectives.

Start by having a conversation about her goals and how she plans to achieve them. Ask her what steps she needs to take, what resources she might need, and what challenges she anticipates along the way. Then, offer your help in whatever way you can. Maybe you can assist with research, connect her with people in your network, or help her brainstorm ideas. The key is to show her that you're not just passively supportive—you're actively invested in her success.

Another important aspect of goal-setting is accountability. When your wife has big dreams, it can be easy to get overwhelmed or to lose motivation along the way. This is where you can step in as her partner and help her stay focused and on track. Check in with her regularly about her progress, offer encouragement when she's feeling stuck, and help her navigate any obstacles that come up. Be that steady presence that keeps her moving forward, even when the road gets tough.

And don't forget to celebrate the milestones along the way. Achieving a big dream doesn't happen overnight—it's a series of small steps, and each one deserves recognition. When your wife reaches a milestone, whether it's completing a course, launching a new project, or even just making progress on a long-term goal, take the time to celebrate with her. Acknowledge the hard work she's put in, and let her know how proud you are of her determination and perseverance.

Balancing Your Dreams and Hers

Now, let's talk about balance. Supporting your wife's dreams doesn't mean putting your own on the back burner—it's about finding a way to balance both of your aspirations in a way that's healthy and sustainable for your relationship. It's about being partners in each other's success and creating a life where both of your dreams can thrive.

Start by having an open and honest conversation about your individual goals and how you can support each other in achieving them. Talk about the challenges you might face, the sacrifices you might need to make, and the ways you can work together to create a balance that works for both of you. The key is to approach this conversation with a mindset of partnership and collaboration, rather than competition or compromise.

Remember, it's not about whose dreams are more important—it's about finding a way to make space for both of your goals in your life together. This might mean taking turns focusing on each other's dreams, or it might mean finding ways to work toward your goals simultaneously. Whatever approach you take, the important thing is to stay committed to supporting each other and to keep the lines of communication open.

And don't forget to be flexible. Life is unpredictable, and there will be times when one person's dreams need to take priority for a while. Maybe your wife has a big opportunity that requires extra time and attention, or maybe you're pursuing a goal that requires more of her support. The key is to be adaptable and to recognize that the balance will shift over time. What's important is that you're both committed to supporting each other, no matter what.

Encouraging Her to Dream Big

One of the most powerful ways you can support your wife is by encouraging her to dream big. It's easy to get caught up in the day-to-day responsibilities of life and to put our dreams on the back burner. But as her partner, you have the unique opportunity to remind her of her potential, to encourage her to aim high, and to support her in going after what she really wants.

Start by helping her overcome any doubts or fears she might have about pursuing her dreams. Maybe she's worried about failing, or maybe she's hesitant to take a risk because of the potential consequences. Be that voice of encouragement that reminds her of her strengths, her talents, and her ability to succeed. Help her see that it's okay to take risks, to step out of her comfort zone, and to go after what she really wants.

And don't be afraid to challenge her to dream even bigger. Sometimes we limit ourselves because we're afraid of aiming too high or because we don't believe we're capable of achieving something great. As her partner, you can help her break through those limitations by encouraging her to think bigger, to set ambitious goals, and to believe in her ability to achieve them. Be that person who sees her potential even when she doesn't, and who pushes her to go after the life she really wants.

Being There for the Journey

Supporting your wife's dreams isn't just about being there for the destination—it's about being there for the entire journey. This means being present, being engaged, and being committed to supporting her through every step of the process.

Be there to listen when she needs to talk, to offer advice when she asks for it, and to provide encouragement when she's feeling discouraged. Show her that you're in this with her, every step of the way, and that you're committed to seeing her succeed. This might mean staying up late to help her with a project, or it might mean just sitting with her and offering comfort when things get tough. Whatever it takes, be there for her, and show her that she's not alone in this journey.

And remember to be patient. Pursuing a dream can be a long and challenging process, and there will be times when progress is slow or when setbacks happen. Be patient with her, and remind her that the journey is just as important as the destination. Help her stay focused on the bigger picture, and remind her that every step forward, no matter how small, is a step in the right direction.

Building a Partnership of Dreams

My brothers, let me leave you with this thought—supporting your wife's dreams is one of the most powerful ways you can show her that you love her. It's about being her partner in the truest sense of the word—someone who's there for her, who believes in her, and who's committed to helping her achieve her goals.

When you support her dreams, you're not just helping her reach her potential—you're building a partnership that's built on love, respect, and a shared vision for the future. You're showing her that her dreams matter, that her happiness and fulfillment are important to you, and that you're in this together, no matter what.

So I challenge you to start supporting your wife's dreams today. Have those conversations, be her biggest cheerleader, make space for her goals in your life together, and encourage her to dream big. Be there for the journey, celebrate the milestones, and stay committed to helping her achieve everything she wants in life.

Because when you support her dreams, you're not just building a stronger, more fulfilling marriage—you're creating a life where both of your dreams can thrive. And that, my friends, is what true partnership is all about.

Navigating Conflict with Grace

Alright, fellas, let's talk about something that's inevitable in every relationship: conflict. Yeah, I know it's not the most comfortable topic, but hear me out. Conflict is a part of life, and it's definitely a part of marriage. No two people can live together, love together, and share their lives without bumping heads every now and then. But here's the thing—how you handle conflict can make all the difference between a marriage that just survives and a marriage that truly thrives.

You see, conflict isn't necessarily a bad thing. In fact, when handled with grace, it can be an opportunity for growth, for understanding, and for deepening the connection between you and your wife. It's not about avoiding disagreements or pretending that everything is always perfect—it's about learning how to navigate those rough waters in a way that strengthens your relationship rather than tearing it apart.

Now, I know that navigating conflict with grace can be tough. It's easy to let emotions take over, to get defensive, or to say things in the heat of the moment that you later regret. But with the right tools and mindset, you can learn to handle conflict in a way that's healthy, constructive, and even healing for your marriage.

We're going to dive into strategies for managing disagreements with your wife in a way that brings you closer together, rather than pushing you apart. We'll talk about how to avoid blame, how to listen with the intention of understanding, and how to work together to find solutions that are fair and respectful. So let's get into it—because when you learn to navigate conflict with grace, you're not just resolving disagreements, you're building a stronger, more resilient marriage.

Understanding the Nature of Conflict

Before we get into the nitty-gritty of conflict resolution, let's take a step back and talk about the nature of conflict itself. Conflict happens when two people have differing needs, wants, or perspectives. It's a natural part of any relationship, and it's not something to be afraid of or to avoid. In fact, conflict can be an important opportunity for growth, both as individuals and as a couple.

The key to navigating conflict with grace is to shift your mindset. Instead of seeing conflict as a threat to your relationship, try to view it as an opportunity to learn more about your wife, to understand her better, and to work together to find solutions that benefit both of you. When you approach conflict with this mindset, it becomes less about winning or losing and more about strengthening your connection.

But let's be real—conflict can be uncomfortable, especially when emotions are running high. It's easy to get caught up in the heat of the moment and to say or do things that you later regret. That's why it's so important to approach conflict with intentionality and mindfulness. By being aware of your own emotions, and by being committed to handling disagreements in a constructive way, you can navigate even the toughest conflicts with grace.

The Importance of Emotional Regulation

One of the most important skills in navigating conflict with grace is emotional regulation. When we're in the middle of a disagreement, it's easy to let our emotions take over. We might feel angry, hurt, frustrated, or defensive, and those emotions can quickly escalate the conflict if we're not careful.

Emotional regulation is about recognizing your emotions, acknowledging them, and then choosing how to respond in a way that's constructive rather than destructive. It's about staying calm, keeping things in perspective, and making a conscious effort to communicate in a way that's respectful and fair.

Now, I'm not saying this is easy—it takes practice. But one of the best things you can do in the midst of a conflict is to take a step back and check in with yourself. Ask yourself, "What am I really feeling right now? And how can I express that feeling in a way that's respectful and constructive?" This simple act of self-reflection can help you avoid saying things in the heat of the moment that you might later regret.

Another important aspect of emotional regulation is taking a break when you need it. If you're feeling overwhelmed or if you notice that the conversation is escalating, it's okay to take a pause. Tell your wife that you need a moment to collect your thoughts and that you'll come back to the conversation when you're feeling calmer. Taking a break doesn't mean you're avoiding the issue—it means you're giving yourself the space to approach it with a clear head and a calm heart.

Listening to Understand

One of the most powerful tools in navigating conflict is listening. But I'm not just talking about hearing the words your wife is saying—I'm talking about truly listening with the intention of understanding. When you listen to understand, you're making a conscious effort to see things from her perspective, to validate her feelings, and to show her that you care about what she has to say.

Listening to understand means putting aside your own agenda, your own need to be right, and your own desire to respond. It's about being fully present in the moment, giving her your undivided attention, and really tuning in to what she's saying—not just the words, but the emotions behind the words.

One of the best ways to practice this is by using active listening techniques. This means reflecting back what she's said to ensure that you've understood her correctly. You might say something like, "So what I'm hearing is that you feel frustrated because I didn't follow through on what I said I would do. Is that right?" This not only shows her that you're listening, but it also gives her the opportunity to clarify if needed.

Another important aspect of listening to understand is acknowledging her feelings. Even if you don't agree with everything she's saying, you can still validate her emotions. You might say, "I can see that this is really upsetting for you, and I understand why you're feeling that way." Validation doesn't mean you're conceding the argument—it just means you're recognizing her experience and showing her that you care about how she feels.

And here's the thing—when you listen to understand, you're not just defusing the conflict, you're also building trust and intimacy in your relationship. You're showing your wife that her thoughts, feelings, and perspectives matter to you, and that you're committed to understanding her, even when you don't see eye to eye. This kind of deep, empathetic listening can transform the way you navigate conflict and can bring you closer together as a couple.

Avoiding Blame and Criticism

Let's talk about blame and criticism—two things that can quickly escalate a conflict and create distance between you and your wife. It's easy to fall into the trap of blaming or criticizing when you're feeling hurt or frustrated, but these behaviors are counterproductive and can cause lasting damage to your relationship.

Blame is about pointing the finger at your partner and making them responsible for the problem. It sounds something like, "This is all your fault," or "You always do this." Blame creates defensiveness and puts your wife on the spot, making it difficult for her to respond constructively. It shifts the focus from solving the problem to assigning fault, which isn't helpful in finding a resolution.

Criticism, on the other hand, is about attacking your partner's character rather than addressing the specific behavior that's bothering you. It might sound like, "You're so selfish," or "You never think about anyone but yourself." Criticism is harmful because it's personal—it attacks who your wife is as a person, rather than focusing on the behavior that needs to change. Over time, repeated criticism can erode your wife's self-esteem and create a sense of resentment and distance in your relationship.

So how do you avoid blame and criticism in the midst of a conflict? It starts with focusing on your own feelings and needs rather than attacking your partner. Use "I" statements to express how you're feeling and what you need, rather than "you" statements that assign blame. For example, instead of saying, "You never help around the house," you might say, "I'm feeling really overwhelmed with the housework, and I could use some help." This approach is more likely to lead to a constructive conversation because it focuses on your experience rather than attacking your wife.

Another strategy is to focus on specific behaviors rather than generalizations. Instead of saying, "You always do this," focus on the specific situation at hand. You might say, "When you didn't call to let me know you'd be late, I felt worried and unimportant." By addressing the specific behavior, you're making it easier for your wife to understand how her actions affected you, and you're opening the door to a productive conversation about how to handle similar situations in the future.

Finding Common Ground

Conflict resolution is all about finding common ground. It's not about winning or losing—it's about working together to find a solution that meets both of your needs. This requires a willingness to compromise, to be flexible, and to approach the situation with an open mind.

One of the best ways to find common ground is to focus on your shared goals and values. What do you both want out of this situation? What's important to both of you? By identifying the common ground, you can shift the focus from your differences to your shared interests, which makes it easier to find a solution that works for both of you.

Let's say, for example, that you're having a disagreement about how to spend your weekends. You want to spend time together as a family, while your wife wants some time to pursue her hobbies. Instead of arguing about whose needs are more important, try to find common ground. You both value quality time together, and you both understand the importance of personal hobbies. From there, you can work together to create a plan that meets both of your needs—maybe you spend Saturday mornings together as a family and give each other time in the afternoon to pursue your individual interests.

Finding common ground also means being willing to compromise. This doesn't mean giving up what's important to you, but it does mean being open to finding a middle ground that works for both of you. Sometimes this means making small sacrifices for the sake of your relationship, and sometimes it means being creative in finding solutions that meet both of your needs.

Apologizing and Forgiving

No matter how hard we try, we're all going to make mistakes from time to time. We're going to say things we don't mean, we're going to hurt each other, and we're going to fall short of our best selves. That's just part of being human. But what's important is how we handle those mistakes when they happen.

Apologizing and forgiving are two of the most powerful tools in conflict resolution. They're about acknowledging our own shortcomings, taking responsibility for our actions, and choosing to let go of resentment and move forward together.

When you've hurt your wife, it's important to apologize sincerely. A genuine apology is about more than just saying "I'm sorry"—it's about taking responsibility for your actions and acknowledging the impact they've had on your wife. A good apology might sound something like, "I'm really sorry for what I said earlier. I realize that I hurt you, and that wasn't my intention. I'm going to work on being more mindful of my words in the future."

And here's the thing—apologizing doesn't make you weak. It doesn't mean you're conceding the argument or admitting that you're entirely at fault. It simply means that you value your relationship more than your pride, and that you're willing to take responsibility for your part in the conflict.

Forgiving, on the other hand, is about letting go of the hurt and resentment that can build up after a conflict. It's about choosing to move forward and to focus on healing and rebuilding your connection. Forgiveness doesn't mean forgetting what happened, and it doesn't mean that the hurt didn't matter. It simply means that you're choosing to let go of the pain and to focus on the future rather than the past.

Forgiveness can be tough, especially when the hurt runs deep. But it's a crucial part of healing and moving forward in your relationship. When you choose to forgive, you're choosing to prioritize your marriage and to focus on rebuilding the trust and intimacy that may have been damaged by the conflict.

Turning Conflict into Growth

Finally, let's talk about how conflict can be an opportunity for growth. When you navigate conflict with grace, you're not just resolving disagreements—you're also learning more about each other, about yourselves, and about your relationship. You're building stronger communication skills, you're deepening your understanding of each other's needs and perspectives, and you're strengthening your bond as a couple.

One of the best ways to turn conflict into growth is to reflect on the experience after the dust has settled. Take some time to talk with your wife about what you both learned from the conflict. What did you learn about her needs and perspectives? What did you learn about yourself and how you handle disagreements? What can you both do differently in the future to navigate conflict more effectively?

This kind of reflection can be incredibly powerful in helping you grow as a couple. It allows you to take a step back, to learn from the experience, and to use that knowledge to strengthen your relationship moving forward.

And here's the thing—when you approach conflict as an opportunity for growth, you're not just resolving disagreements—you're also building a marriage that's resilient, that's capable of weathering the storms of life, and that's grounded in love, respect, and understanding.

Choosing Grace Over Grudge

My brothers, conflict is an inevitable part of marriage, but how you handle it is what truly matters. When you choose to navigate conflict with grace, you're choosing to prioritize your relationship, to honor your wife's feelings and perspectives, and to work together to find solutions that strengthen your bond.

It's not about avoiding disagreements or pretending that everything is always perfect—it's about approaching conflict with a mindset of growth, of understanding, and of love. It's about listening to understand, avoiding blame and criticism, finding common ground, and being willing to apologize and forgive when needed.

And remember, conflict isn't something to be feared—it's an opportunity to learn, to grow, and to deepen your connection with your wife. So the next time you find yourselves in the midst of a disagreement, I challenge you to choose grace over grudge, to choose understanding over defensiveness, and to choose growth over stagnation.

Because when you navigate conflict with grace, you're not just resolving disagreements—you're building a marriage that's strong, resilient, and grounded in love. And that, my friends, is the kind of marriage that can weather any storm and come out stronger on the other side.

Cultivating Patience and Understanding

Alright, gentlemen, let's dive into something that every single one of us has to work on—patience. Whether it's waiting in line at the grocery store or dealing with a frustrating situation at work, we all have moments where our patience is tested. But when it comes to marriage, patience isn't just a nice-to-have—it's a necessity. It's one of those qualities that, when cultivated, can transform your relationship from something that's merely good into something that's truly great.

Now, let's be honest here. Patience doesn't come naturally to everyone, and that's okay. We live in a world where everything is instant—instant coffee, instant messaging, instant results. We've been conditioned to expect things to happen quickly, and when they don't, it's easy to get frustrated. But marriage isn't about quick fixes. It's about the long haul, the day-to-day commitment to love and understand your partner, especially during the tough times.

Let's explore what it means to cultivate patience and understanding in your marriage. We'll talk about why patience is so crucial, how to practice empathy when things get tough, and ways to keep perspective when it feels like everything is falling apart. Because here's the truth, fellas: a marriage that's built on patience and understanding is a marriage that can weather any storm. So let's get into it.

The Power of Patience in Marriage

Let's start by talking about what patience really means in the context of marriage. It's more than just biting your tongue when you're irritated or counting to ten when you're frustrated. Patience is about giving your wife—and yourself—the time and space to grow, to change, and to be human. It's about recognizing that neither of you is perfect and that's okay.

Think about it this way: in a marriage, you're two imperfect people trying to build a life together. There are going to be moments when you don't see eye to eye, when you get on each other's nerves, or when things just don't go the way you planned. Patience is what helps you navigate those moments without letting them derail your relationship.

Patience is also about resisting the urge to react impulsively. When your wife says something that rubs you the wrong way or when she's going through something that's affecting your relationship, it's easy to react out of frustration. But reacting impulsively often leads to regret—saying things you don't mean, escalating conflicts, or shutting down emotionally.

Instead, patience allows you to take a step back, to breathe, and to approach the situation with a calm, steady hand. It's about choosing to respond rather than react. When you respond with patience, you're creating an environment where both you and your wife can express yourselves openly, without fear of judgment or escalation.

And here's the thing—patience isn't just about handling the big stuff, like major life changes or conflicts. It's about the small, everyday moments too. It's about being patient when she's running late, when she's stressed out, or when she's dealing with something that's affecting her mood. It's about recognizing that sometimes she just needs a little extra grace, a little extra understanding, and a little extra love.

Understanding Through Empathy

Now, let's talk about empathy—the ability to understand and share the feelings of another person. Empathy is one of the most powerful tools you have in your marriage because it allows you to connect with your wife on a deeper level. It's about putting yourself in her shoes, seeing things from her perspective, and feeling what she's feeling.

But empathy isn't always easy, especially when you're in the middle of a tough time. When you're stressed, tired, or frustrated, it can be hard to tune into your wife's emotions. But this is exactly when empathy is most needed—when things aren't going smoothly, and when you're both feeling the strain.

One of the keys to practicing empathy is active listening, which we talked about earlier in this book. When your wife is expressing herself, whether she's upset, worried, or just venting, your job is to listen—not to fix, not to offer solutions, but to truly listen. Hear her out, and try to understand what she's going through from her perspective.

Sometimes, empathy means acknowledging that you don't fully understand what she's feeling, but you're still there for her. You might say something like, "I can see that you're really struggling with this, and I'm here to support you, even though I might not fully get it." This kind of response shows her that you're making an effort to connect with her emotions, even if you can't completely relate.

Another important aspect of empathy is recognizing that your wife's feelings are valid, even if you don't agree with them. There will be times when you see things differently, and that's okay. What's important is that you acknowledge her feelings and treat them with respect. This doesn't mean you have to agree with everything she says, but it does mean that you honor her emotional experience as real and significant.

Practicing Patience During Tough Times

Let's be real—marriage isn't always a walk in the park. There will be tough times, whether it's financial stress, health issues, family conflicts, or just the everyday pressures of life. It's during these times that your patience and understanding will be put to the test.

One of the most important things to remember during tough times is that it's not you against your wife—it's you and your wife against the problem. When you approach challenges as a team, you're reinforcing the idea that you're in this together, no matter what life throws your way.

But staying patient during tough times isn't easy. Stress can bring out the worst in us, and it's easy to take out your frustrations on the person closest to you. This is where self-awareness comes into play. Pay attention to your own emotional state and be mindful of how you're communicating with your wife. Are you snapping at her because you're stressed about work? Are you shutting down because you're feeling overwhelmed? Recognizing these patterns is the first step in breaking them.

When you feel your patience wearing thin, take a moment to pause and reflect. What's really going on here? Are you upset with your wife, or is something else triggering your frustration? Sometimes, just taking a few deep breaths and giving yourself a moment to cool down can make all the difference.

Another important aspect of practicing patience during tough times is managing your expectations. Life doesn't always go according to plan, and neither does marriage. When you're facing challenges, it's important to adjust your expectations and to be flexible in how you approach the situation.

For example, if your wife is going through a particularly stressful time at work, she might not have the energy to be as present or engaged as she usually is. Rather than getting frustrated or feeling neglected, try to be understanding. Recognize that this is a temporary situation and that your support can make a big difference in helping her through it.

Keeping Perspective

Perspective is everything when it comes to cultivating patience and understanding in your marriage. It's about seeing the bigger picture, recognizing what truly matters, and not getting caught up in the small stuff.

When you're in the middle of a disagreement or when things aren't going well, it's easy to lose sight of the bigger picture. You might find yourself fixating on the problem at hand, feeling like it's the end of the world. But taking a step back and keeping things in perspective can help you navigate these moments with more grace and composure.

One way to keep perspective is to remind yourself of what you love and appreciate about your wife. When you're feeling frustrated or impatient, take a moment to think about all the things she does that make your life better. Focus on the qualities that drew you to her in the first place, and remember that the current challenge is just one small part of your overall relationship.

Another way to keep perspective is to think about the long-term goals of your marriage. What are you and your wife working toward together? What are the values and priorities that you both share? When you keep these long-term goals in mind, it's easier to navigate the bumps in the road without letting them derail your relationship.

It's also important to recognize that tough times don't last forever. Whatever challenges you're facing right now, they will pass. And when they do, your marriage will be stronger for having weathered them together. Keeping this in mind can help you stay patient and understanding, even when things aren't going smoothly.

The Role of Compassion

Compassion is a close cousin to empathy, but it goes a step further. While empathy is about understanding and sharing the feelings of another person, compassion is about wanting to alleviate their suffering and being moved to take action.

In marriage, compassion is about recognizing when your wife is struggling and stepping up to support her, even if it means putting your own needs and desires on hold. It's about being there for her in both big and small ways, showing her that you care about her well-being and that you're committed to helping her through whatever challenges she's facing.

Compassion also means being gentle with your wife when she's going through a tough time. Maybe she's not handling things the way you would, or maybe she's reacting in a way that's frustrating to you. But instead of criticizing or judging her, compassion invites you to approach her with kindness and understanding.

One of the best ways to cultivate compassion in your marriage is to ask yourself, "How would I want to be treated if I were in her shoes?" This simple question can help you shift your perspective and approach your wife with more empathy and care.

Patience with Yourself

While we've been talking a lot about being patient with your wife, it's equally important to be patient with yourself. Marriage is a journey, and you're not always going to get it right. There will be times when you lose your patience, when you say or do something you regret, or when you struggle to understand your wife's perspective. And that's okay.

What matters is that you're committed to growing, to learning, and to becoming a better partner every day. This means being patient with yourself as you navigate the ups and downs of marriage. It means giving yourself grace when you make mistakes and recognizing that growth takes time.

One of the most powerful things you can do is to approach your marriage with a growth mindset. This means seeing challenges and setbacks as opportunities for learning and improvement, rather than as failures. When you embrace a growth mindset, you're more likely to be patient with yourself and with your wife, knowing that every experience—good or bad—is an opportunity to grow closer and stronger together.

Building a Foundation of Patience and Understanding

Patience and understanding aren't just nice qualities to have in a marriage—they're the foundation upon which a strong, lasting relationship is built. When you cultivate these qualities, you're creating an environment where both you and your wife can thrive, where you can navigate challenges with grace, and where your love can deepen over time.

Remember, patience isn't about suppressing your feelings or ignoring your needs—it's about giving your marriage the time and space it needs to grow. It's about responding with empathy and compassion, even when things are tough, and keeping perspective when the road gets rocky.

And most importantly, patience is about being kind to yourself and to your wife. It's about recognizing that you're both human, that you're both doing your best, and that it's okay to stumble along the way. What matters is that you keep showing up, that you keep choosing to love each other, and that you keep working together to build the kind of marriage you both deserve.

So my brothers, as you continue on this journey of loving your wife better, remember that patience and understanding are your greatest allies. Embrace them, practice them, and watch as they transform your marriage into something truly beautiful. Because at the end of the day, a marriage built on patience and understanding is a marriage that can withstand anything—and that's the kind of love story worth living.

Building Trust Through Transparency

Hey, my brothers, today we're going to talk about one of the most vital foundations of any successful marriage—trust. Trust isn't something you can just put on a checklist and mark off once it's built. No, trust is a living, breathing thing. It's built brick by brick through your actions, words, and how you show up every single day. And here's the kicker: it can be broken in a moment but takes a lot of time, effort, and intention to rebuild. Trust is what makes your wife feel safe, secure, and confident in your relationship. And one of the most powerful tools you have in building that trust is transparency.

Now, when we talk about transparency, we're talking about being open and honest in all areas of your relationship. That's not just about the big things like finances or major life decisions, but the little things too—your thoughts, your feelings, your fears, your mistakes. Transparency is about letting your wife see the real you, even when it's uncomfortable or when you think you might be judged.

So let's dig into this concept of building trust through transparency, because once you understand how powerful it is, you'll see just how transformative it can be for your marriage.

Why Trust Matters So Much

First, let's get clear on why trust is so crucial in a marriage. Trust is the foundation of intimacy, love, and connection. Without it, everything else in your relationship is on shaky ground.

When your wife trusts you, she feels safe. And when she feels safe, she's able to open up, to be vulnerable, to share her heart with you. That's when true intimacy happens.

Trust isn't just about believing that your partner won't betray you. It's about believing that your partner has your back, that they're honest with you, and that they'll do what they say they're going to do. Trust is about reliability, consistency, and truth. It's knowing that you can count on each other, no matter what.

But trust doesn't happen overnight. It's something that's built over time, through your actions, your words, and your commitment to being transparent. And that's where transparency comes into play. When you're transparent with your wife, you're saying, "I have nothing to hide. I trust you with my truth." And that, my friends, is how you start building a rock-solid foundation of trust in your marriage.

The Power of Transparency

Transparency is about more than just telling the truth—it's about being proactive in your honesty. It's about making the choice to be open, even when it's uncomfortable, even when it's easier to keep something to yourself. When you're transparent, you're not just avoiding lies—you're actively choosing to let your wife into your world.

So what does transparency look like in a marriage? It's about sharing your thoughts and feelings, even when they're messy or complicated. It's about being honest about your mistakes and taking responsibility for your actions. It's about communicating openly about your needs, your desires, and your boundaries. And it's about being upfront about the things that matter, whether it's your finances, your plans for the future, or your past.

Transparency is powerful because it creates a deep sense of trust and security. When your wife knows that you're being open with her, she doesn't have to worry about hidden agendas or secrets. She can relax into the relationship, knowing that what she sees is what she gets. That kind of security allows her to be more open with you, creating a positive cycle of trust and transparency that strengthens your connection.

But transparency isn't just about the big stuff—it's about the small, everyday moments too. It's about being honest about your feelings when you've had a tough day at work. It's about sharing your thoughts on a decision you're both trying to make. It's about being upfront when something is bothering you, rather than letting it fester and create distance between you.

And let me tell you something, brothers—transparency takes courage. It's not always easy to be open, especially when you're dealing with something that makes you feel vulnerable. But the more you practice transparency, the stronger your marriage will become. Because when you're willing to be transparent, you're showing your wife that you trust her enough to let her see the real you.

Being Transparent About Your Feelings

One of the most important areas where transparency is crucial is in sharing your feelings. Now, I know for some of us, this can be tough. We've been conditioned to keep our emotions in check, to tough it out, to not let anyone see when we're struggling. But here's the thing—your wife wants to know what's going on inside of you. She wants to be part of your inner world, to understand what you're feeling and why.

When you're transparent about your feelings, you're letting your wife in on what's really happening in your heart and mind. Maybe you're feeling stressed about work, or you're worried about a family issue, or you're just feeling down for no particular reason. Whatever it is, sharing those feelings with your wife helps her understand you better, and it helps you process those emotions in a healthy way.

Being transparent about your feelings also means being honest when something is bothering you in your relationship. Maybe there's a recurring issue that's been bothering you, or maybe you're feeling disconnected. Whatever it is, it's important to talk about it openly, rather than letting it build up and create resentment.

When you're transparent about your feelings, you're not just sharing information—you're creating an opportunity for deeper connection and understanding. You're inviting your wife to see the real you, and you're showing her that you trust her with your emotions. That kind of openness can transform your relationship, turning moments of vulnerability into moments of deep connection.

Owning Your Mistakes

We all make mistakes. It's part of being human. But how you handle those mistakes can make a huge difference in your marriage. When you mess up—and you will, because we all do—it's crucial to own up to it. This is where transparency becomes absolutely vital.

Owning your mistakes means being upfront about what you've done, taking responsibility, and being willing to make amends. It's about saying, "I messed up, and I'm sorry," rather than trying to cover it up or shift the blame. When you're transparent about your mistakes, you're showing your wife that you're committed to honesty and integrity in your relationship.

But owning your mistakes isn't just about admitting when you've done something wrong—it's also about being willing to learn from those mistakes. It's about recognizing the impact of your actions and taking steps to ensure it doesn't happen again. When you approach your mistakes with a mindset of growth and learning, you're turning a negative experience into an opportunity to strengthen your marriage.

And here's the thing—when you own your mistakes, you're also giving your wife permission to do the same. You're creating a culture of transparency in your marriage, where both of you feel safe to be honest about your flaws and your missteps. This kind of environment fosters trust and allows you to navigate challenges together, rather than letting them drive a wedge between you.

The Importance of Intentions

Another key aspect of transparency is being clear about your intentions. This means communicating openly about what you want, what you need, and where you see your relationship going. When you're transparent about your intentions, you're setting the stage for mutual understanding and alignment in your marriage.

Being transparent about your intentions is especially important when it comes to major decisions in your life. Whether it's your career plans, your financial goals, or your dreams for the future, it's important to share those intentions with your wife. This helps ensure that you're both on the same page and that you're working together toward the same goals.

But transparency about your intentions isn't just about the big stuff—it's also about the everyday things. Maybe you have plans to spend the weekend working on a project, or you're thinking about making a change in your routine. Whatever it is, being open about your intentions helps avoid misunderstandings and ensures that your wife feels included in your plans.

When you're transparent about your intentions, you're showing your wife that you respect her enough to be honest about what you want and where you're headed. This kind of openness fosters trust and helps you build a relationship that's based on mutual understanding and shared goals.

Financial Transparency

Let's talk about one of the biggest sources of conflict in many marriages—finances. Money can be a touchy subject, but it's also one of the most important areas where transparency is crucial. Financial transparency means being open and honest about your financial situation, your spending habits, and your financial goals.

Being financially transparent with your wife helps build trust because it shows that you're committed to being responsible and accountable when it comes to money. It also ensures that you're both on the same page when it comes to financial decisions, which can help prevent misunderstandings and conflicts down the road.

Financial transparency isn't just about sharing the numbers—it's also about sharing your financial mindset. This means being open about your attitudes toward money, your financial priorities, and any concerns or anxieties you may have. When you're transparent about your financial mindset, you're creating an opportunity for deeper understanding and alignment in your marriage.

If you're struggling with financial transparency, it might be helpful to start by setting aside some time to talk openly about your finances. This could involve reviewing your budget together, discussing your financial goals, or just sharing your thoughts and feelings about money. The key is to approach the conversation with an open mind and a willingness to listen and learn from each other.

Transparency and Boundaries

While transparency is crucial, it's also important to understand that it works best when it's balanced with healthy boundaries.

Boundaries are about knowing where to draw the line and respecting each other's needs for space and privacy. Being transparent doesn't mean you have to share every single thought or detail—sometimes it's about knowing what's appropriate to share and what's not.

Transparency and boundaries go hand in hand. When you have healthy boundaries, you're better able to be transparent without feeling overwhelmed or exposed. Boundaries help ensure that your transparency is rooted in respect and mutual understanding, rather than feeling like an obligation or a chore.

It's important to talk openly with your wife about your boundaries and to listen to her needs and boundaries as well. This creates a framework for transparency that's respectful and supportive, allowing you to be open and honest with each other while still maintaining your individuality and personal space.

Building Trust Over Time

Building trust through transparency is a process—it doesn't happen overnight. It's about consistently showing up with honesty, integrity, and openness in your marriage. Over time, these small, consistent acts of transparency build a strong foundation of trust that can withstand the challenges and stresses of life.

As you work on being more transparent in your marriage, remember that it's okay to take it one step at a time. You don't have to overhaul your entire communication style overnight. Instead, focus on being more open in your everyday interactions, whether it's sharing a thought that you'd usually keep to yourself, admitting when you've made a mistake, or talking openly about your intentions for the future.

And remember, my brothers, transparency isn't just about what you say—it's about how you live. It's about aligning your words with your actions and being the kind of partner your wife can trust with her heart. When you live with transparency, you're not just building trust—you're building a marriage that's rooted in love, respect, and mutual understanding.

The Strength of a Transparent Marriage

As we wrap up this chapter, I want you to take a moment to reflect on the power of transparency in your marriage. Transparency is more than just a tool for building trust—it's a way of life. It's about being open, honest, and authentic in all areas of your relationship, and it's about creating a space where your wife feels safe, valued, and understood.

When you commit to transparency, you're making a powerful choice to build a marriage that's rooted in trust and integrity. You're showing your wife that you have nothing to hide, that you trust her with your truth, and that you're committed to being the best partner you can be.

Remember, building trust through transparency isn't always easy. It takes courage, vulnerability, and a willingness to be open even when it's uncomfortable. But the rewards are worth it. A marriage built on transparency is a marriage that can weather any storm, a marriage where both partners feel secure, and a marriage where love can truly flourish.

So, my brothers, I encourage you to embrace transparency in your marriage. Start small, be consistent, and watch as your marriage grows stronger, deeper, and more connected than ever before. Because at the end of the day, a marriage built on trust and transparency is a marriage that can stand the test of time—and that's the kind of love story worth fighting for.

Sharing Responsibilities

Hey, brothers, let's get real for a second. When you hear the word "partnership," what comes to mind? Is it two people working together, side by side, sharing the load, and supporting each other? Or do you think more about one person doing most of the heavy lifting while the other steps in occasionally? Now, I want you to think about your marriage and ask yourself—what does your partnership look like?

Marriage is a true partnership, and sharing responsibilities is at the heart of that partnership. It's about recognizing that both you and your wife have a role to play in keeping your lives running smoothly—whether it's managing the household, raising kids, or planning for the future. When you share responsibilities, you're saying to your wife, "I see you, I value you, and I'm here to support you." It's about being an equal partner, not just in words, but in action.

But here's the truth—many of us have been conditioned to believe that certain responsibilities fall to one partner more than the other. Maybe you grew up in a home where your mom did all the cooking and cleaning while your dad handled the finances and yard work. Or maybe you've internalized the idea that as long as you're bringing home a paycheck, you're doing your part.

Well, my brothers, it's time to shake off those outdated ideas and step into a new way of thinking. Sharing responsibilities is about more than just dividing tasks—it's about creating harmony in your marriage. It's about ensuring that your wife doesn't feel overwhelmed or unsupported, and that both of you feel like true partners in every aspect of your life together.

So, let's dive into what it means to share responsibilities in your marriage, why it's so important, and how you can start making changes today that will bring more balance, fairness, and love into your relationship.

Understanding the Concept of Equality in Partnership

First things first, let's talk about what it means to be an equal partner. Equality in partnership doesn't mean that you and your wife have to do the exact same tasks in equal amounts. It's not about splitting everything down the middle like a pizza. Instead, it's about recognizing that both of you bring unique strengths, abilities, and preferences to the table—and finding a way to share the load in a way that feels fair and balanced to both of you.

Equality in partnership is about respect. It's about acknowledging that your wife's time, energy, and contributions are just as valuable as yours. Whether she's working outside the home, managing the household, raising your children, or doing a combination of these things, her efforts are crucial to the success and happiness of your family.

When you approach your marriage as an equal partnership, you're making a commitment to show up for each other, to support each other, and to share the responsibilities that come with building a life together. This mindset shift is key because it sets the foundation for everything else we're going to talk about in this chapter.

The Invisible Load: What Your Wife Carries

Now, let's get into something that a lot of us don't even realize is happening—what's often called the "invisible load." The invisible load refers to all the mental and emotional work that goes into managing a household and caring for a family. It's the constant juggling of tasks, the mental checklist that never seems to end, the planning, the worrying, and the organizing.

For many women, the invisible load is a significant source of stress and exhaustion. Even in marriages where responsibilities are shared, it's often the wife who takes on the bulk of this mental and emotional labor. And the thing is, because it's invisible, it's easy to overlook or underestimate.

So what does the invisible load look like? It's things like remembering to schedule doctor's appointments, keeping track of the kids' activities, planning meals, noticing when the household supplies are running low, and making sure everyone's needs are met. It's the behind-the-scenes work that keeps everything running smoothly, but that often goes unnoticed and unappreciated.

If you want to be a true partner to your wife, it's crucial to start recognizing the invisible load and finding ways to share it. This doesn't just mean helping out more with tasks around the house—it means taking on some of the mental and emotional work as well. It means being proactive, rather than waiting for your wife to ask for help. It means stepping up and taking responsibility for the things that need to get done, rather than assuming that she's got it covered.

Sharing Household Chores: A Team Effort

Alright, let's get down to the nitty-gritty—household chores. Cleaning, cooking, laundry, dishes, grocery shopping, taking out the trash—these are the tasks that keep your home functioning day in and day out. And while they might not be glamorous, they are essential.

In too many households, the burden of household chores falls disproportionately on women. Even in households where both partners work full-time, studies show that women still do the majority of the housework. This imbalance can lead to resentment, frustration, and burnout for your wife—and that's the last thing you want in your marriage.

So how do you start sharing household chores more equally? It starts with communication. Sit down with your wife and have an honest conversation about how the chores are currently divided and how she's feeling about it. Ask her what tasks feel overwhelming or unfair to her, and be open to hearing her perspective without getting defensive.

Once you've had that conversation, work together to come up with a plan that feels fair and balanced to both of you. This might mean dividing certain tasks equally, or it might mean taking on different responsibilities based on your strengths and preferences. The key is to approach it as a team effort, where both of you are committed to making sure the household runs smoothly without one person bearing the brunt of the work.

And let me tell you something—when you start sharing household chores, you're not just lightening your wife's load. You're also showing her that you value and respect her time and energy. You're showing her that you see her as an equal partner, and that you're willing to do your part to create a harmonious and happy home.

Parenting: Equal Responsibility, Equal Joy

If you have children, parenting is another area where sharing responsibilities is absolutely crucial. Raising kids is one of the most rewarding, challenging, and important things you'll ever do—and it's something that should be shared equally between you and your wife.

For too long, society has perpetuated the idea that women are naturally better suited for parenting, while men are the "helpers." But the truth is, parenting is a shared responsibility, and both parents have an equally important role to play in their children's lives.

Sharing parenting responsibilities means being fully involved in all aspects of raising your kids, from changing diapers and feeding them as babies, to helping with homework, attending school events, and being there for the big and small moments as they grow. It means being just as committed to your role as a parent as your wife is, and being there to support her as she supports you.

But sharing parenting responsibilities isn't just about the tasks—it's also about sharing the emotional labor of parenting. This means being involved in the decision-making, the planning, and the worrying. It means being there to comfort your kids when they're upset, to celebrate their successes, and to guide them through their challenges.

And here's the thing—when you share parenting responsibilities, you're not just supporting your wife. You're also building a deeper connection with your children. You're showing them that both of their parents are there for them, that they are loved and supported by both mom and dad. And that kind of connection is priceless.

Financial Responsibilities: A Joint Venture

Let's talk money. Financial responsibilities are another critical area where sharing the load is essential for a healthy, balanced marriage. Whether you're managing day-to-day expenses, paying bills, budgeting, or planning for the future, finances are a joint venture that requires both partners to be involved.

In some marriages, one partner takes on most of the financial responsibilities—whether it's earning the majority of the income, managing the budget, or making financial decisions. But this kind of imbalance can lead to tension and stress, especially if one partner feels overwhelmed or left out of the financial picture.

Sharing financial responsibilities means working together to create a budget, plan for future expenses, and make decisions about how to use your money. It means being transparent about your financial situation, your goals, and your concerns. And it means both of you taking responsibility for managing your finances in a way that supports your family's needs and dreams.

If one of you is more knowledgeable about finances, that's great—use that knowledge to educate and support each other, rather than taking on all the responsibility yourself. Financial literacy is important for both partners, and by sharing financial responsibilities, you're ensuring that both of you are equipped to make informed decisions that benefit your family.

And remember, sharing financial responsibilities isn't just about managing the money—it's also about sharing the emotional load that comes with it. Money can be a major source of stress, especially when things are tight or when you're facing big financial decisions. By sharing this responsibility, you're supporting each other emotionally as well as financially, and that's key to maintaining a strong, healthy partnership.

Communication: The Key to Sharing Responsibilities

At the heart of sharing responsibilities is communication. You can't share the load if you're not talking openly and honestly about what needs to be done, how you're feeling, and what support you need from each other. Communication is the bridge that connects you and your wife as you work together to build a balanced, harmonious life.

So how do you improve communication around sharing responsibilities? Start by making it a regular part of your conversations. Rather than waiting until things reach a breaking point, make it a habit to check in with each other about how things are going. Ask your wife how she's feeling, and be open about how you're feeling too. Talk about what's working well and what could be improved, and be willing to make adjustments as needed.

It's also important to approach these conversations with empathy and understanding. Remember, sharing responsibilities isn't about keeping score or trying to prove who's doing more—it's about working together as a team. Listen to your wife's concerns with an open heart, and be willing to step up and make changes if she's feeling overwhelmed or unsupported.

And finally, be proactive. Don't wait for your wife to ask for help—look for opportunities to step in and share the load. Whether it's taking on a task that you know she doesn't enjoy, or offering to handle something that's been stressing her out, your willingness to be proactive will go a long way in showing her that you're committed to being an equal partner.

The Benefits of Sharing Responsibilities

When you start sharing responsibilities more equally in your marriage, you're going to notice some powerful benefits. First and foremost, you're going to create a stronger, more harmonious partnership with your wife. When she sees that you're committed to sharing the load, she's going to feel more supported, valued, and respected—and that's going to bring you closer together.

You're also going to reduce stress and burnout for both of you. When responsibilities are shared more equally, neither partner has to bear the brunt of the work alone. This creates a more balanced, peaceful environment at home, where both of you can thrive.

And let's not forget the impact on your kids. When they see both parents sharing responsibilities, they're learning important lessons about equality, teamwork, and respect. You're setting an example for them that will shape their own relationships in the future, and that's a legacy worth creating.

Finally, sharing responsibilities can reignite the love and passion in your marriage. When both partners feel supported and valued, there's more room for connection, intimacy, and joy. You're not just partners in managing your household—you're partners in life, and that's something to celebrate.

Stepping Up as an Equal Partner

So, brothers, as we wrap up this chapter, I want you to take a moment to reflect on what it means to be an equal partner in your marriage. Sharing responsibilities isn't just about doing your fair share of the work—it's about showing your wife that you're committed to building a life together, side by side. It's about creating a partnership that's rooted in respect, balance, and mutual support.

As you move forward, I encourage you to start taking action today. Look for opportunities to share the load more equally, to step up and support your wife, and to create a more balanced, harmonious partnership. It's not always going to be easy, and there will be times when you'll have to have tough conversations and make adjustments. But the rewards are worth it.

When you share responsibilities, you're not just lightening your wife's load—you're strengthening your marriage. You're creating a partnership that's built on equality, respect, and love, and that's the foundation for a truly fulfilling life together.

So step up, be an equal partner, and watch as your marriage becomes stronger, more joyful, and more connected than ever before. Because at the end of the day, sharing responsibilities isn't just about getting things done—it's about building a life that you and your wife can be proud of, together.

Prioritizing Intimacy

Alright, brothers, we've talked a lot about communication, trust, and partnership in this book so far. But now we're going to dive into something that is just as important—intimacy. And I'm not just talking about the physical side of things here. Intimacy is about so much more than just sex. It's about connection, closeness, and understanding your partner on a deep level. It's about feeling seen, heard, and valued in your marriage.

When we think about intimacy, most of us go straight to the physical. And yes, physical intimacy is a beautiful, essential part of any marriage. But to build a strong, lasting relationship, you need to nurture all dimensions of intimacy—emotional, physical, and intellectual. It's about creating a bond that goes beyond the surface, one that keeps you and your wife close no matter what life throws your way.

So, we're going to explore these different dimensions of intimacy. We'll talk about what they mean, why they're important, and how you can prioritize them in your marriage. By the end of this chapter, you'll have the tools and insights you need to deepen your connection with your wife, ensuring that your intimacy remains strong and vibrant throughout your marriage.

Understanding Emotional Intimacy

Let's start with emotional intimacy, which is often the foundation for everything else in a relationship. Emotional intimacy is about sharing your thoughts, feelings, and experiences with your partner in a way that fosters closeness and understanding. It's about being vulnerable, open, and honest with each other. When you have strong emotional intimacy, you feel connected to your wife on a deep level—you know each other's hopes, dreams, fears, and insecurities.

But here's the thing, brothers—emotional intimacy doesn't just happen on its own. It takes work, commitment, and a willingness to be vulnerable. Many of us have been taught that showing emotion is a sign of weakness, especially as men. We've been told to "man up" and keep our feelings to ourselves. But in a marriage, this mindset can be damaging. If you want to build strong emotional intimacy with your wife, you need to be willing to let your guard down and share your true self with her.

So how do you cultivate emotional intimacy? It starts with communication. And I'm not just talking about surface-level conversations here—I'm talking about deep, meaningful discussions where you really open up to each other. Share your fears, your dreams, your struggles, and your triumphs. Be honest about how you're feeling, even if it's uncomfortable. When you share your inner world with your wife, you're inviting her into your life in a way that strengthens your bond.

It's also important to create a safe space for your wife to share her emotions with you. Listen to her without judgment, and let her know that you're there to support her no matter what. When both of you feel safe to express your emotions openly, you create a strong foundation of trust and closeness that can weather any storm.

And remember, emotional intimacy isn't just about the big, deep conversations—it's also about the little moments of connection throughout the day. It's the hug you give her when she's had a rough day, the way you look into her eyes and really listen when she's talking, the small gestures that show you care. These moments might seem small, but they add up to create a strong emotional bond that keeps you close.

Nurturing Physical Intimacy

Now, let's talk about physical intimacy. Physical intimacy is often what people think of first when they hear the word "intimacy," but as we've discussed, it's just one piece of the puzzle. However, it's still a crucial part of a healthy marriage, and it deserves your attention and effort.

Physical intimacy is about more than just sex—it's about touch, affection, and the physical connection that you share with your wife. It's the way you hold her hand, the way you kiss her goodnight, the way you cuddle up together on the couch. These small acts of physical closeness are powerful ways to maintain your bond and show your love for each other.

Of course, sexual intimacy is also an important part of physical intimacy, and it's something that requires care, attention, and communication. But let's be real, brothers—life can get in the way sometimes. Work, kids, stress, and exhaustion can all take a toll on your sex life. And that's okay. The key is to prioritize physical intimacy in a way that works for both of you, even when life gets busy.

So how do you keep the spark alive in your marriage? First, make time for physical intimacy. This might mean scheduling date nights, setting aside time for each other after the kids are in bed, or simply making an effort to be affectionate throughout the day. It's about making physical closeness a priority, rather than letting it fall by the wayside.

Second, communicate openly with your wife about your needs, desires, and boundaries. Talk about what feels good for both of you, what you'd like to explore, and how you can keep your physical connection strong. And remember, physical intimacy is a two-way street—it's just as important to listen to your wife's needs and desires as it is to express your own.

Finally, don't underestimate the power of non-sexual touch. A hug, a kiss on the forehead, a gentle touch on the arm—these small gestures of physical affection can be incredibly powerful in maintaining your bond. They remind your wife that you're there for her, that you love her, and that you're connected on a deep, physical level.

Fostering Intellectual Intimacy

Alright, brothers, we've talked about emotional and physical intimacy, but there's another dimension that's just as important—intellectual intimacy. Intellectual intimacy is about connecting with your wife on a mental level. It's about sharing ideas, interests, and passions, and engaging in deep, meaningful conversations that stimulate your minds and keep you connected.

Intellectual intimacy is often overlooked in discussions about intimacy, but it's a powerful way to strengthen your bond with your wife. When you share your thoughts, ideas, and interests with each other, you're creating a deeper understanding and appreciation for each other's minds. You're connecting on a level that goes beyond the physical and emotional, and that's incredibly important for a lasting relationship.

So how do you foster intellectual intimacy in your marriage? First, make an effort to engage in meaningful conversations with your wife. Talk about your passions, your goals, your opinions on current events, or even the book you're reading. Ask her about her thoughts and listen with an open mind. These conversations can be a great way to learn more about each other, and they can keep your relationship feeling fresh and exciting.

Second, find activities that you can enjoy together that stimulate your minds. This might mean taking a class together, working on a project, or simply discussing a topic that interests both of you. The key is to find ways to engage your minds together, to challenge each other, and to grow together intellectually.

Finally, support each other's intellectual growth. Encourage your wife to pursue her interests, and be her biggest cheerleader when she's learning something new or taking on a new challenge. When you support each other's intellectual growth, you're showing that you value each other's minds just as much as you value each other's hearts and bodies.

Balancing the Dimensions of Intimacy

Now that we've covered the different dimensions of intimacy, let's talk about how to balance them in your marriage. Each dimension—emotional, physical, and intellectual—plays a crucial role in creating a strong, lasting connection with your wife. But the key is to find a balance that works for both of you.

The truth is, every marriage is different. What works for one couple might not work for another, and that's okay. The important thing is to communicate openly with your wife about what you both need in terms of intimacy, and to be willing to make adjustments as needed.

For some couples, emotional intimacy might be the foundation of their relationship, while for others, physical intimacy might be the most important. The key is to recognize that all three dimensions are important, and to make an effort to nurture each one in your marriage.

One way to do this is to make intimacy a regular part of your conversations with your wife. Check in with each other about how you're feeling emotionally, physically, and intellectually connected. Talk about what's working well and what could be improved, and be willing to make changes to ensure that both of you feel fulfilled and satisfied in your relationship.

And remember, intimacy isn't a one-time thing—it's something that needs to be nurtured and prioritized throughout your marriage. It's about making a commitment to stay close, to stay connected, and to keep the love alive, no matter what life throws your way.

The Role of Vulnerability in Intimacy

Before we wrap up this chapter, I want to touch on something that's crucial to all dimensions of intimacy—vulnerability. We've talked about vulnerability before, but it's worth revisiting here because it's such an essential part of creating and maintaining intimacy in your marriage.

Vulnerability is about being open, honest, and authentic with your wife. It's about sharing your true self with her, even when it's uncomfortable. It's about letting her see your fears, your insecurities, and your weaknesses, as well as your strengths and successes.

When you're vulnerable with your wife, you're creating a space where true intimacy can flourish. You're showing her that you trust her with your deepest self, and that you're willing to let her in, even when it's scary. And when she's vulnerable with you, she's doing the same.

But here's the thing—vulnerability isn't easy. It takes courage, especially if you've been taught that showing emotion is a sign of weakness. But the truth is, vulnerability is a strength. It's what allows you to connect with your wife on a deep, meaningful level. It's what allows you to create a marriage that's built on trust, love, and true intimacy.

So, brothers, I encourage you to embrace vulnerability in your marriage. Be willing to let your guard down, to share your true self with your wife, and to create a space where she can do the same. When you do, you're going to find that your connection becomes stronger, deeper, and more fulfilling than ever before.

Prioritizing Intimacy in Your Marriage

As we wrap up this chapter, I want you to take a moment to reflect on the different dimensions of intimacy in your marriage—emotional, physical, and intellectual. How are you doing in each of these areas? Are there areas where you could improve? Are there things you could do to deepen your connection with your wife?

Remember, intimacy is about more than just physical closeness—it's about connecting on every level. It's about feeling seen, heard, and valued in your relationship. It's about creating a bond that goes beyond the surface, one that keeps you and your wife close no matter what life throws your way.

So, brothers, I challenge you to prioritize intimacy in your marriage. Make time for meaningful conversations, for physical closeness, and for intellectual connection. Be vulnerable with your wife, and create a space where she can be vulnerable with you. And most importantly, make a commitment to nurture your intimacy throughout your marriage, no matter what.

Because at the end of the day, intimacy is what keeps your marriage strong. It's what keeps you connected, even when life gets tough. It's what allows you to build a relationship that's built on love, trust, and true connection. And that's something worth fighting for.

So go out there and prioritize intimacy in your marriage, brothers. Your wife deserves it, and so do you.

The Joy of Giving Without Expecting

Alright, my brothers, we're getting to a powerful truth that can transform not only your marriage but your entire life: the joy of giving without expecting anything in return. Now, I know that sounds like a tall order. We're often conditioned to think that relationships are a two-way street—if I do this, then I expect that in return. But what if I told you that the true magic, the true depth of love, lies in giving purely, selflessly, without any expectation of return?

This chapter is about embracing that mindset, about finding joy and fulfillment in the act of giving to your wife simply because you love her, because you want to see her happy, and because it's the right thing to do. When you give without expecting anything back, you create a kind of love that is pure, that is deep, and that binds you and your wife together in a way that's unshakeable.

So, let's dive in. We're going to talk about what it means to give selflessly, why it matters, and how you can start practicing this in your marriage. By the end of this chapter, you'll have a new perspective on love, one that will not only enrich your relationship with your wife but also bring you a sense of joy and fulfillment that goes beyond anything you've ever known.

Understanding Selfless Giving

First things first, let's break down what it means to give selflessly. Selfless giving is about doing something for your wife without any strings attached. It's about making her a priority, about seeing her needs, desires, and well-being as important as—if not more important than—your own. It's about giving from a place of love, without looking for praise, without expecting a thank you, and without keeping score.

Now, this doesn't mean you're a doormat or that you let yourself be taken advantage of. Selfless giving is not about losing yourself or neglecting your own needs. It's about understanding that in a loving, healthy marriage, when you give selflessly, you're actually enriching both of you. You're creating a cycle of positivity, where your acts of love inspire love in return, even if that return doesn't come in the exact way you might expect.

Selfless giving might look like staying up late to help your wife with something, even when you're tired. It might mean taking on extra chores so she can have a break, or surprising her with something small that you know she loves, just because. It's about those little acts of kindness that show her, day in and day out, that she is loved, cherished, and valued.

The Power of Small Gestures

Let's talk about the power of small gestures, because sometimes we think that giving has to be something grand, something big and bold. But the truth is, it's often the small, consistent acts of love that make the biggest difference in a marriage.

Think about it: how do you feel when your wife does something small for you, like making your favorite meal, leaving a sweet note in your bag, or just giving you a hug when you need it most? Those moments stick with you, right? They make you feel loved and appreciated. The same goes for her.

So, brothers, I want you to start paying attention to the small things. Notice what your wife loves, what makes her smile, what brings her comfort. Then, start incorporating those things into your daily routine. Maybe it's making sure there's coffee ready for her in the morning, or sending her a text in the middle of the day just to say you're thinking about her. Maybe it's running her a bath after a long day, or picking up her favorite snack on your way home.

These small gestures are powerful because they show your wife that she's on your mind, that you're thinking about her even in the little moments. They're a way of saying, "I see you, I care about you, and I want to make you happy." And when you do these things without expecting anything in return, you're giving her a gift that's truly from the heart.

The Ripple Effect of Selfless Love

One of the most beautiful things about selfless giving is the ripple effect it creates in your marriage. When you give to your wife without expecting anything back, you're setting the tone for your relationship. You're creating an atmosphere of love, kindness, and generosity. And more often than not, that energy comes back to you in ways you might not expect.

When your wife feels loved and cherished by your selfless acts, she's going to want to reciprocate. She's going to feel more connected to you, more valued, and more inclined to show you love in return. And before you know it, you've created a cycle of giving, where both of you are pouring into each other without keeping score, without tallying who's done what.

This doesn't mean you're always going to get back exactly what you give, or that you should expect your wife to match you gesture for gesture. The beauty of selfless giving is that it's not about tit-for-tat. It's about creating a relationship where love flows freely, where both partners feel supported, valued, and cherished.

And even when the giving doesn't come back in the way you might expect, you'll find that the act of giving itself is fulfilling. You'll discover that there's a deep joy in making your wife happy, in seeing her smile, in knowing that you've made her day a little bit better. That's the kind of joy that can't be measured, that goes beyond anything material or superficial.

Practicing Selfless Giving in Tough Times

Now, let's be real—there are going to be times when selfless giving feels hard. Maybe you're stressed, tired, or going through a rough patch in your marriage. Maybe you feel like you've been giving a lot and not getting much back in return. In those moments, it can be tempting to pull back, to stop giving because you feel like it's not worth it, or because you're not being appreciated.

But here's the thing, brothers: selfless giving is most powerful when it's hardest to do. It's easy to give when everything's going great, when you're feeling loved and supported. But when things are tough, when you're feeling disconnected or unappreciated, that's when selfless giving can make the biggest impact.

In those moments, I want you to remember why you're giving in the first place. You're giving because you love your wife, because you want to see her happy, because you're committed to your marriage. When you give from that place, you're not just doing something nice—you're making a powerful statement about your commitment to your relationship.

And often, it's in those tough times that your selfless acts of love can help turn things around. When your wife sees that you're still there for her, that you're still committed to showing her love even when things are hard, it can help rebuild trust, connection, and intimacy. It can be the spark that reignites the flame in your marriage, reminding both of you of the love that brought you together in the first place.

The Joy of Giving Freely

So, what's the payoff? What do you get out of giving without expecting anything in return? The answer might surprise you. The joy that comes from giving freely is one of the most fulfilling feelings you can experience. When you give purely out of love, you're tapping into a source of joy that's deep, lasting, and incredibly powerful.

This joy comes from knowing that you've made a positive impact on your wife's life. It comes from seeing her smile, from knowing that you've made her day a little brighter. It comes from the sense of fulfillment that comes with giving from the heart, from the knowledge that you're doing something good, something that matters.

But beyond that, the joy of giving freely also comes from the way it transforms your own heart. When you give without expecting anything back, you're practicing gratitude, humility, and love. You're training yourself to focus on the positive, to find happiness in the act of giving itself, rather than in what you might get in return.

And the beautiful thing is, this joy is contagious. When you experience the joy of giving freely, it spreads to other areas of your life. You start to see opportunities to give in other relationships, in your work, in your community. You become more attuned to the needs of others, more willing to step up and make a difference.

In this way, the joy of selfless giving becomes a way of life. It's not just something you do in your marriage—it's a mindset, a way of approaching the world with love, kindness, and generosity. And that, brothers, is a powerful thing.

Overcoming the Challenges of Selfless Giving

Now, I know that selfless giving isn't always easy. We all have moments when we feel drained, when we're struggling to give anything at all. Maybe you're dealing with stress at work, financial pressures, or health issues. Maybe you're feeling disconnected from your wife, or you're going through a tough time in your marriage.

In those moments, it's important to remember that selfless giving doesn't mean giving until you're completely depleted. It's not about sacrificing your own well-being or burning yourself out. Instead, it's about finding ways to give that are sustainable, that nourish both you and your wife.

One way to do this is to focus on quality rather than quantity. You don't have to give grand gestures all the time—in fact, sometimes the smallest acts of love are the most powerful. It's about being thoughtful, about finding ways to show your love that don't require huge amounts of time, energy, or resources.

Another key is to take care of yourself so that you have the capacity to give. Selfless giving starts with self-care. When you're feeling good, when you're taking care of your own needs, you'll have more to give to your wife. So make sure you're taking time for yourself, getting enough rest, eating well, and managing stress. When you're in a good place, you'll find it easier to give from a place of love and generosity.

Finally, it's important to communicate with your wife about what you need in order to continue giving. Selfless giving doesn't mean you don't have needs or that you should ignore your own well-being. If you're feeling drained or overwhelmed, talk to your wife about it. Let her know what's going on and work together to find ways to support each other.

The Reward of a Deeper Connection

When you embrace selfless giving, when you make it a regular practice in your marriage, you're going to notice something powerful: your connection with your wife will deepen. When you give without expecting anything in return, you're creating a relationship that's built on love, trust, and mutual respect. You're building a bond that's strong, resilient, and deeply fulfilling.

This deeper connection is the reward of selfless giving. It's the knowledge that you and your wife are truly partners, that you're in this together, that you're both committed to making each other's lives better. It's the feeling of knowing that you're loved for who you are, not for what you can give, but simply because you're you.

And when you have that kind of connection, when you and your wife are both giving freely and selflessly, you're going to find that your marriage is stronger, happier, and more fulfilling than ever before. You'll find that you're able to navigate challenges with grace, to support each other through tough times, and to celebrate the good times with joy.

Embracing the Joy of Selfless Giving

As we wrap up this chapter, I want you to take a moment to reflect on the joy of selfless giving. Think about the times when you've given to your wife without expecting anything in return—how did that make you feel? How did it impact your relationship? And how can you bring more of that joy into your marriage?

Remember, brothers, selfless giving is not about being a martyr or sacrificing your own happiness. It's about finding joy in the act of giving, about creating a relationship where love flows freely, without strings attached. It's about building a marriage that's built on love, trust, and mutual respect.

So, I challenge you to embrace the joy of selfless giving in your marriage. Start with small gestures, focus on quality, and take care of yourself so that you have the capacity to give. And most importantly, give from a place of love, without expecting anything in return. When you do, you'll find that the rewards are greater than anything you could have imagined. You'll find that your marriage is stronger, your connection is deeper, and your life is more fulfilling.

Because at the end of the day, the joy of selfless giving is the joy of true love. It's the joy of knowing that you're making a difference in your wife's life, that you're creating a marriage that's built to last, and that you're living a life filled with love, kindness, and generosity. And that, my brothers, is something worth striving for.

Growing Together, Not Apart

Alright, my brothers, we've come a long way together. We've talked about love, vulnerability, trust, patience, and so much more. And now, we've arrived at our final chapter—a chapter that might be the most important one of all. Because while it's crucial to build a strong foundation, to nurture intimacy, and to give selflessly, there's one thing that will truly determine the longevity and health of your marriage: your ability to grow together, not apart.

Marriage isn't static. It's not something you "arrive" at and then you're done. No, marriage is a journey, an ongoing process of evolution and change. You and your wife are both going to grow and change over the years—that's a given. The real question is: will you grow together or will you grow apart?

We're going to dive deep into what it means to grow together as a couple. We'll talk about supporting each other's personal development, about navigating the inevitable changes that life throws your way, and about ensuring that your relationship not only survives these changes but thrives because of them.

By the end of this chapter, you'll have the tools and the mindset you need to keep your marriage strong, healthy, and full of love, no matter how much you and your wife evolve over time.

Embracing Change in Marriage

Let's start by talking about change. Now, change is a scary word for a lot of people, especially when it comes to relationships.

We often hear things like "we just grew apart" or "he's not the same person I married," and that can create fear around the idea of change. But here's the truth, brothers: change is inevitable. It's going to happen whether we like it or not. The real challenge is not to resist change, but to embrace it and use it as a catalyst for growth.

When you got married, you and your wife were probably different people than you are today. Think back to who you were when you first met—your hopes, your dreams, your goals. Chances are, those things have shifted over time. Maybe you've both gone through career changes, maybe you've become parents, maybe you've faced challenges that you never saw coming. All of these experiences change us. They shape who we are and how we see the world.

And that's okay. In fact, it's more than okay—it's a beautiful thing. Because it means you're living, you're evolving, and you're continuing to grow. The key is to make sure that as you grow as individuals, you're also growing together as a couple.

The Importance of Personal Growth

Before we talk about growing together, we need to address the importance of personal growth. Because here's the thing: in order to grow together, you first need to be committed to growing yourself. Personal growth is not just about improving yourself for your own sake—it's also about becoming the best partner you can be.

So ask yourself: are you committed to your own growth? Are you actively working on becoming the best version of yourself?

Are you open to learning new things, to challenging your old beliefs, to stepping outside of your comfort zone? Because that's what it's going to take to grow alongside your wife.

Personal growth can take many forms. It might mean pursuing your passions, going back to school, starting a new hobby, or working on your physical and mental health. It might mean seeking therapy or coaching to work through your past issues, or simply being more mindful and present in your daily life.

Whatever form it takes, personal growth is crucial because it keeps you engaged with life, it keeps you evolving, and it keeps you interesting—not just to yourself, but to your wife as well. When you're committed to your own growth, you're bringing new energy, new ideas, and new perspectives into your marriage. And that's something that can keep your relationship vibrant and exciting, even after many years together.

Supporting Each Other's Growth

Now that we've talked about the importance of personal growth, let's turn our attention to supporting each other's growth as a couple. Because while it's important to grow as individuals, it's equally important to support your wife's growth and to ensure that your growth doesn't pull you apart.

So how do you do that? How do you make sure that as you and your wife evolve, you're doing it in a way that strengthens your relationship rather than weakens it?

First and foremost, it starts with communication. You need to be talking to your wife about your goals, your dreams, your fears, and your challenges. You need to be open about the changes you're going through and be willing to listen to the changes she's experiencing as well.

Let me tell you, one of the biggest mistakes couples make is assuming that they know everything about each other. You might think you know your wife inside and out, but the truth is, she's constantly changing, just like you are. And if you're not keeping up with those changes, if you're not talking about them and exploring them together, you're going to find yourselves drifting apart.

So make it a priority to check in with each other regularly. Ask her about her goals and dreams. What does she want to accomplish in the next year? The next five years? What challenges is she facing? What new passions or interests has she discovered? And don't just ask these questions once—make it a regular part of your relationship to check in and support each other's growth.

Growing Through Challenges

Let's be real—growth doesn't always come easy. Sometimes, growth comes through challenges, through difficult times, and through experiences that push you to your limits. But here's the thing: those challenges, as tough as they may be, are often the very things that bring you closer together.

When you face challenges as a couple, whether it's a financial crisis, a health issue, or a conflict in your relationship, you have two choices. You can let those challenges drive a wedge between you, or you can use them as an opportunity to grow together.

One of the most powerful ways to grow together through challenges is by being there for each other. When your wife is going through a tough time, she needs to know that you're in her corner, that you're her rock, and that you're not going anywhere. And when you're facing challenges, you need to be open with her about what you're going through and let her be there for you as well.

But it's not just about being there for each other—it's also about learning from the challenges you face. When you go through something difficult, take the time to reflect on what you've learned from it. How has it changed you? How has it changed your relationship? And how can you use those lessons to grow closer together in the future?

Evolving Together as a Couple

As you and your wife grow and change, your relationship will naturally evolve as well. The key is to make sure that you're evolving together, not apart. So what does that look like in practice?

First, it means being intentional about your relationship. Don't just assume that your marriage will stay strong without effort. Just like anything else in life, a strong marriage requires time, energy, and attention. So make your marriage a priority. Set aside time to connect with each other, to talk about your goals and dreams, and to nurture your relationship.

Second, it means being flexible and adaptable. As you and your wife evolve, your relationship will need to evolve as well. What worked for you when you were first married might not work for you now. Maybe your communication styles have changed, or maybe you need to find new ways to connect as your lives have become busier or more complicated.

Be willing to adapt and change as your relationship evolves. Don't be afraid to try new things, to let go of old habits that no longer serve you, and to embrace the new dynamics that come with growth.

Finally, it means growing in the same direction. This doesn't mean you have to have all the same goals and interests as your wife—after all, you're still two separate individuals. But it does mean that you're aligned in your values, in your vision for the future, and in your commitment to each other.

Make sure that as you grow, you're checking in with each other to ensure that you're still on the same page. Are your goals aligned? Are you both working towards the same vision for your future? If not, what adjustments do you need to make to get back in sync?

Creating a Vision for Your Future

One of the most powerful ways to ensure that you're growing together as a couple is to create a shared vision for your future. This is about more than just setting goals—it's about imagining the life you want to build together and then taking intentional steps to make that vision a reality.

So take some time to sit down with your wife and talk about your vision for the future. What do you both want your life to look like in the next 5, 10, or 20 years? What are your dreams for your career, your family, your personal growth, and your relationship? And most importantly, how can you support each other in making that vision a reality?

This shared vision is like a roadmap for your relationship. It gives you a sense of direction and purpose, and it helps you stay focused on what really matters. And as you work towards this vision together, you'll find that your relationship becomes stronger, more resilient, and more deeply connected.

Staying Connected Through the Years

As the years go by, it's easy to get caught up in the busyness of life. Careers, kids, responsibilities—they can all take a toll on your relationship if you're not careful. But if you want to grow together and not apart, you need to be intentional about staying connected.

One of the best ways to do this is to create rituals that keep you connected. These don't have to be big, elaborate gestures—sometimes, the smallest things make the biggest difference. Maybe it's a weekly date night, a morning coffee ritual, or a nightly check-in where you talk about your day. Whatever it is, make sure it's something that you both look forward to and that helps you stay connected.

Another important aspect of staying connected is continuing to have fun together. Don't let the stresses of life steal the joy from your relationship. Keep finding ways to laugh, to play, and to enjoy each other's company. Whether it's trying a new hobby together, taking a weekend getaway, or just being silly at home, make sure you're finding ways to keep the fun and joy alive in your relationship.

And finally, keep the romance alive. Don't let the spark fade just because you've been together for a long time. Keep surprising each other, keep flirting with each other, and keep finding ways to show your love and affection. Remember, romance isn't just for the honeymoon phase—it's something that should continue throughout your entire marriage.

The Power of Reflection

As you and your wife continue to grow together, it's important to take time to reflect on your journey. Look back on how far you've come, on the challenges you've overcome, and on the growth you've experienced as individuals and as a couple.

Reflection is powerful because it helps you see the progress you've made and the strength of your relationship. It also helps you identify any areas where you might need to make adjustments or improvements.

So make reflection a regular part of your relationship. Take time every so often to sit down with your wife and talk about how things are going. What's working well? What could be better? What changes do you need to make to continue growing together?

This practice of reflection will help you stay connected, aligned, and focused on your shared vision for the future. It will also help you appreciate the journey you've been on together and the love that continues to grow between you.

The Journey of Growing Together

As we wrap up this chapter and this book, I want you to take a moment to reflect on everything we've talked about. Marriage is a journey, a journey of growth, of love, and of connection. It's a journey that requires commitment, effort, and a willingness to evolve—both as individuals and as a couple.

Growing together is not always easy, but it's one of the most rewarding experiences you can have. It's about building a life together, supporting each other's dreams, and creating a love that deepens and matures over time. It's about staying connected, staying aligned, and staying committed to each other, no matter what life throws your way.

So, my brothers, I challenge you to embrace this journey of growing together. Commit to your own growth, support your wife's growth, and make your relationship a priority. Create a shared vision for your future, stay connected through the years, and never stop working on your relationship.

When you do, you'll find that your marriage becomes a source of strength, joy, and fulfillment. You'll find that you and your wife are not just surviving the ups and downs of life, but thriving together, growing closer with each passing year. And you'll find that your love, far from fading over time, continues to grow, to evolve, and to flourish—stronger and more beautiful than ever before.

Because at the end of the day, that's what marriage is all about: growing together, not apart. It's about building a life filled with love, connection, and shared dreams. And that, my brothers, is a journey worth taking.

Don't miss out!

Visit the website below and you can sign up to receive emails whenever Malcolm Carter publishes a new book. There's no charge and no obligation.

https://books2read.com/r/B-A-DMCLC-XKHZE

BOOKS 2 READ

Connecting independent readers to independent writers.

About the Author

Malcolm Carter is a distinguished scholar and relationship expert specializing in the dynamics of marital communication and emotional intelligence. With a background in psychology, Carter combines academic insight with practical wisdom to help men foster deeper, more meaningful connections with their partners. His work is dedicated to empowering individuals to create lasting, fulfilling relationships grounded in understanding and respect.